COOK

—WITH—

TOFU

COOK

—WITH—

TOFU

—CHRISTINA CLARKE—

AVON
PUBLISHERS OF BARD, CAMELOT, DISCUS AND FLARE BOOKS
A Madison Press Book

COOK WITH TOFU is an original publication of Avon Books. This work has never before appeared in book form.

AVON BOOKS
A division of
The Hearst Corporation
959 Eighth Avenue
New York, New York 10019

To
Lorraine, Charles,
Linn, Katie, Marcia,
and
Toni-Sensei
for your clear-seeing
kindness and support.

Contents

Acknowledgments

I would like to express my gratitude to the following people who so generously gave me support and assistance during the writing of this book.

To the people who asked me to consider writing a tofu cookbook in the first place and whose support and good humor have been constant throughout this entire project: designer, illustrator and cook extraordinaire Marcia Smith, Hugh Brewster, Albert Cummings, President of Madison Press Books in Toronto, and Greg Weaver, owner of The Lotus Café in Rochester, New York.

In Rochester during the early days of this project, many helpful suggestions and sources for further exploration were provided by Norman Holland and Andy Schecter of Northern Soy, as well as by Taeko Heiser and Yasue Uchida.

To the Soycrafters Association of North America, especially to Richard Leviton, President of SANA and editor of its magazine *Soyfoods,* for making much useful material available. To all soycrafters and people related to the soyfoods industry in their various capacities who responded to my request for a business or institutional listing. I sincerely regret having no space to include them, but wish to express my thanks for the words of encouragement that often accompanied these replies and always brightened my day. Thanks especially to Carol Hargadine, Tom Moore, Mary Anderson and Mara Devine.

To Dr. John Erdman of the University of Illinois Food Science Department and Dr. Joseph Rackis of the United States Department of Agriculture Northern Regional Research Center who took the time to answer many questions concerning soybean chemistry and nutrition during the 1980 Soyfoods Showcase conference in Urbana, Illinois, and to Dr. Norman Gambill and Jack Wallace.

For additional technical assistance, information and advice, thanks to Don Nelson and Madeline Fox of the New England Soy Dairy, Walt Henzi of Gilroy Foods, Inc., Hillary Landau of Breezy

Morning Herbs, Walter Kellison and Dorothy Wood of Frontier Cooperative Herbs, Luke Lukoskie and Yvonne of Island Spring, Inc., and Ed Shorer.

And a special thanks to my collaborators in the kitchen, Martha and Jay Thompson, Marcy Apfelbaum and Marcia Smith. Working with them has been a continual learning experience for me. Their recipes are the heart of this cookbook, and I truly could not have written it without them.

To the Rochester Zen Center, first of all for having introduced me to tofu cooked in Western dishes, and also for its generous donation of a number of its most popular tofu recipes. And to the following individuals and restaurants who also donated recipes: Bill Anderson, Mary Anderson, Ron Beck, Jaqueline Borek, Janet Cashin, Lorraine Clarke, Carroll Dougherty, Tucker Held, Barbara Lakeberg, Nina Livingston, Mitzi Piker, Jennifer Taylor, Linn Underhill, Jane Williamson, The Hungry Hunza in Portland, Maine, Soja Soyfood Café and Delicatessen in Toronto, Canada, the Regular Restaurant and The Lotus Café, both in Rochester, New York.

To Angela Kessler who so ably coordinated the testing program, for her good humor, sense of organization and dependability. And finally to the testers themselves, all of whom dutifully followed recipes and registered their comments including helpful hints for improvements which were gratefully incorporated: Trisha Baker, Jackie and John Borek, Lynne Boyd and Patrick Weygint, Joellen Chase, Dennis and Carol Clarke, Lorraine and Charles Clarke, Tracy and Kem Clarke, Gerry and Ann Knigge-Dartt, Amy Davis, Didi and Owen Dinsmore, Susan and Mark Donovan, Carroll Dougherty and Earl Lepper, Susan Dregely, Patsy Friend, Cindy Furlong and Peter Mitchell, Joyce and Stuart Glick, Carol Gordon, Marge Hammer and family, Paul and Mary Hetland, Barry and Judy Keesan, Karla Knight, Debbie and Paul Kuhl, Jessie Haigh, Bill and Nina Livingston, Joan Lyons, Rusty and Beth Madden, Rafe and Rose Martin, Karen Miki and family, Marjorie Oi and family, Noël Phillips and Phil Zimmerman, Margaret Polk, Marion Rigney, Sonja and David Kjolhede Sachter, Jack and Judy Sternberg Spula, Bill and Susan Stone, Mary and Allen Temple and family, Jim and Shirley Thompson, and Mary Gail Walker. And to Joe Anarella, Margaret Howe, Janet Bates and Lee Miller a special thanks for your very adventurous natures and constructive comments.

To William Shurtleff and Akiko Aoyagi for the trail-blazing work they have done and continue to do through their books and The Soyfoods Center, as well as for their sincere interest, helpful hints and encouragement.

To designer John Lee and illustrator Marcia Smith for their very sensitive work from which the written words have benefitted so much. In this regard, thanks also to Carol Inouye of Avon Books.

To editor Shelley Tanaka who clearly saw what needed to be done to make this book more accessible to as many people as possible. It is very much better for her part in it.

To Page Cuddy of Avon Books for her pertinent questions and considerable experience which she so generously shared. And to typist Steve Beren who even during my most discouraged times remained optimistic.

And last but not least, to my family and many unnamed friends whose support did not falter even during those times of high pressure when my moods would swing most drastically.

To all, my thanks for this opportunity to work together.

C. C.
January, 1981

Note:
Unfortunately, we were unable to include a list of soyfood outlets, restaurants and delicatessens, food distributors, related businesses and institutions in this edition, but plan to do so in the future. If you wish to be included, please send the following information to Christina Clarke, *c/o Madison Press Books, The Coach House, 149 Lowther Avenue, Toronto, Ontario, Canada M5R 3M5:*
a) the name of your business or institution,
b) your address (include zip or postal code),
c) your telephone number (include area code),
d) the name of a person to contact and a description of your business or institution's involvement with soyfoods.
   Your comments and suggestions concerning this book will also be much appreciated. Thank you.

Introduction

A few months before I began writing this book, I was standing at the counter in The Lotus Café, Rochester's Soy Delicatessen and Restaurant, waiting for my tofu burger and cup of tea when a nicely dressed woman came in. She walked up to the delicatessen section and began looking at the different products with great interest. When she looked up and saw me watching her she said, smiling, "I have to see what new goodies they've come out with this week."

We began to talk, and the woman told me that she had learned of The Lotus Café through an article in the Rochester paper. She and her husband had been intrigued by the idea of a chocolate mint pie made with tofu, an ingredient they had only encountered previously in Chinese and Japanese restaurants.

They came to The Lotus Café, tried the pie, and liked it so much that they took one home along with the recipe brochure that was being handed out in the shop. After going through these recipes, they started experimenting on their own.

When I asked her if her neighbors were as enthusiastic about tofu as she and her husband semed to be, she replied that until recently they had not shared their discovery of this new food with their friends. There was still something "a little weird" attached to eating it. But this changed.

"One night we invited our best friends over for supper. I didn't serve a tofu dish, but the meal was good, and after we finished eating, the talk turned to other good foods, and I mentioned the article about tofu and The Lotus Café. I said that we had been so intrigued that we decided to drop by one afternoon and try a piece of that tofu chocolate mint pie. Our friends started laughing. 'We did, too,' they said. And then it all came out. They'd been eating more and more tofu, too, but weren't telling anyone either. Ever since then we haven't felt weird about using tofu. Aren't people funny? And isn't it great how new things catch on?"

This is not an isolated case of enthusiasm. My own taste for tofu developed in much the same way. I, too, could hardly believe that I had once been so hesitant to communicate my enthusiasm for this remarkable food.

Tofu can be used by anyone, a fact that is confirmed by the growing number of people who are being attracted to this simple but highly versatile food. It has been featured in magazines and periodicals, from *Family Circle* to *Cuisine* and *Gourmet*. Even the *Wall Street Journal* has given it favorable front-page coverage. Although many of us may have first heard it called bean curd or soy cheese, its Japanese name, "tofu," is beginning to sound as familiar to North Americans as "pizza" and "yogurt," two foods which also seemed foreign to many of us not so long ago.

Like the soybean from which it is produced, tofu is a complete protein, or one which contains all the essential amino acids. But, whereas cooked soybeans have a digestibility rate of 68%, tofu is 95% digestible. With a usable protein content equal to that of chicken, an 8-oz. serving can provide 27% of the adult male's daily protein requirement. Combined with grains, eggs, cheese, seeds, and nuts, its usable protein content increases. It has no cholesterol, is low in calories and sodium, and is relatively free of chemical toxins or additives. What's more, tofu and soymilk are good sources of calcium and are recommended for those who are allergic to dairy products.

To people whose concerns are not health-oriented, but center on the culinary possibilities that tofu offers, this food provides constant surprises. "This quiche is made with tofu??! No cream? It's so light and moist!" is a reaction I've experienced over and over again. Blended with water, juices or broths, tofu can be used in a variety of thicknesses and can match the consistency of light or heavy cream. Its ability to pick up seasonings of any kind make it ideally suited for desserts, as well as main dishes. Used in baked goods it has a satisfying moistening effect. It can be deep-fried, boiled or baked, and when pressed to remove some of its water content, it will be firm enough to be barbecued on a spit.

Lovers of Italian foods will find that tofu can be substituted easily for ricotta cheese or meat. There are also those who simply enjoy a freshly made cake of tofu with soy sauce. Its uses are as diverse as the people who use it.

Many of us are concerned about rising food prices. Here, too, tofu does not disappoint. Of the protein sources available today it is one of the least expensive. In a supermarket or grocery store its cost is approximately three-fifths that of hamburger, and making tofu in your home cuts this cost in half again. The process is not only simple, but allows you to obtain tofu in its freshest and most subtly sweet state.

In the United States soybeans are used primarily to feed livestock raised for meat consumption. It takes from fourteen to twenty pounds of soybeans to make one pound of beef. In this time of world food crisis, many North Americans feel the need and responsibility to discourage this form of waste, and are learning to derive their protein from sources other than meat.

These are only some of the reasons tofu shops and soy dairies are springing up all over this continent. Tofu's journey from China through Japan to North America has taken nearly two thousand years. The method for its preparation is said to have been discovered in China about 164 B.C. and is thought to have reached Japan around the eighth century A.D. In this country tofu has been made commercially since the turn of the century by Chinese and Japanese immigrants. Until recently it had been used mainly in their homes and restaurants and had attracted little notice elsewhere.

With the appearance of *The Book of Tofu* by William Shurtleff and Akiko Aoyagi in late 1975, non-oriental Americans began to recognize the remarkable qualities of this food and to make it themselves. The authors included not only oriental recipes, but also recipes that used tofu in traditional Western dishes. They also discussed in detail how one might open a tofu shop in this country. Many of the tofu shops established by non-Orientals since then have been inspired by *The Book of Tofu* and by personal encouragement from the authors themselves.

"It's the way we began," says Greg Weaver, a former partner in Rochester's Northern Soy Tofu Company and now owner of The Lotus Café. "We read *The Book of Tofu* and started making tofu at home. Soon we were making it a couple of times a week for the local food co-op and the Zen Center where many of us first ate tofu used in Western recipes. The business has grown steadily. Rochester was ready for soyfoods, and the city has been a great place for us to be located.

"There's a concern for better nutrition on all levels here. We've done demonstrations in schools, and some of them are now using tofu. Church and civic groups, supermarkets and department stores have asked us to come in and share what we've learned about using tofu, tempeh, and other soyfoods in American cooking."

Wegmans, the local supermarket chain that first carried Northern Soy's tofu, was persuaded to do so by one of its food brokers. On a trip to Japan he had seen the importance of tofu as a staple in the Japanese diet. When he returned and found that there was a shop in Rochester making fresh tofu, he persuaded Wegmans to carry it.

It took a while to catch on, but Wegmans did not withdraw its support during the initial breakthrough period. Now all the major supermarkets in the Rochester area are selling tofu.

"When tofu began to take hold in the supermarkets and grocery stores," Greg continues, "we needed to have more contact with the public. The restaurant has made that possible. One of our main concerns has always been to show people how tofu can fit into any diet and provide an inexpensive source of protein."

"Our experience here in Toronto has been similar to that of The Lotus Café in Rochester," says Mary Anderson, a partner in Soja Soyfood Café and Delicatessen. "We wanted our restaurant to show people how adaptable soyfoods are to just about anyone's diet.

"Toronto being such an international city has provided us with great opportunities to use tofu in different cuisines. Each week we use tofu or tempeh in recipes from a particular country. It's not a question of forcing tofu into the recipes just so that we can say it's there. Once you figure out how best to use it in a particular dish, it seems like it always belonged there.

"We're happy when people want to try cooking with tofu on their own. That's why we sell cookbooks and have a deli in the restaurant. I heard that The Lotus Café's customers bring in new recipes they have developed at home. Well, we're starting to get that here, too."

In the course of writing this book I have talked with many people involved in soyfoods. They share similar experiences. So it is not astounding to me that tofu is an increasingly common sight in supermarkets and food stores.

People are trying tofu, often first mixed with meat, eggs or cheese. They are finding that it is not only versatile and nutritious, but also easy to use. Even preparatory techniques such as draining, pressing and squeezing will add little to the time and effort you will spend cooking a meal.

I hope this book will help you to begin exploring the many different ways you can use tofu in your diet, and that these recipes will simply be a starting point for your own culinary creativity. You may even want to try making your own tofu at home.* All the recipes in this cookbook have been tested, not only by people who are experienced in cooking with tofu, but also by people who have never cooked with tofu before. Their comments and suggestions have been most helpful, and their enthusiasm has been a real source of encouragement. In the end we all share in inviting *you* to cook with tofu, too.

*For instructions on making tofu at home, see *The Book of Tofu* by William Shurtleff and Akiko Aoyagi, Autumn Press, 1975, or Ballantine, 1979. Tofu-making kits are available from Tree of Life, P.O. Box 76, Bodega, California 94922 or from The Soyfoods Center, P.O. Box 234, Lafayette, California 94549.

Tofu for All Occasions:
(Some Sample Menus)

A Quick Nutritious Breakfast

Hot Miso Broth (p. 61)
Tofu Scrambled Eggs (p. 106)
Whole Wheat Toast

A Breakfast/Brunch for Company

Baked French Toast (p. 107) with Fresh Strawberries and
   Sweet Poppy Dressing (p. 103)
Coffee or Tea

Lunchbox Special

Sandwiches with Deviled Tofu (p. 37) or Spinach Vegetable
   Spread (p. 40)
Raw Vegetable Sticks
Raisins and Nuts

A Hot Lunch That Even Kids Will Love

Soup of Your Choice
Tofuburgers I or II (pp. 74 to 75) with the Works
Tofu Cheese Cake (p. 191) with Fresh Fruit

A Delicious Light Luncheon

Chilled Cucumber Soup
Open-Faced Luncheon Sandwiches (p. 73)
Crisp Green Salad
Almond Apple Tart (p. 195)

A Quick After-Work Supper

Pan-fried Tofu Sticks (p. 110) with Tartar Sauce (p. 99) or
Tangy Dipping Sauce (p. 100)
Steamed Broccoli with Lemon Butter
Fresh Fruit and Pineapple Cashew Spread (p. 42)

A Special Meal to Serve to Friends

Clear Vegetable Soup
Green Salad with Marinated Vegetables
Crispy Beer Batter Nuggets with Mustard Sauce (p. 174)
Maple Walnut Pudding (p. 186) with Marinated Fruit

Surprised by Guests?

Mung Bean Sprout Salad with Ginger Dressing (p. 83)
Spicy Braised Bean Curd (p. 111) with Rice or Noodles
Snow Peas
Sherbet

A Festive Holiday Dinner

Creamed Pumpkin or Squash Soup
Tossed Vegetable Salad with Vinaigrette Dressing
Potato Spinach Roulade with Parmesan Butter Sauce (p. 158)
Cauliflower with Slivered Almonds and Drawn Butter
Cranberry Relish
Croissants
Steamed Apple Pudding (p. 198)

A Late-Night Supper

Tofu Latkes (p. 134) with Tofu Lemon Cream (p. 99),
Sour Cream or Hot Applesauce
Herbal Tea

Buying and Storing Tofu

These days, tofu is sold in three ways: in bulk, packed in water in plastic tubs, and in vacuum packages. The pre-packaged containers will list the soybeans, water and the coagulant used – generally calcium sulfate or nigari (see *Glossary*) – and often nutritional information. There should be a stamped date to indicate the tofu's freshness.

Tofu in Bulk
Tofu is often sold this way in tofu shops and soyfood delicatessens, oriental food markets, and food co-operatives. In some of these places, your tofu will be packaged for you in cardboard containers: in others, you may be expected to bring your own containers.

Cover the tofu with water, and change the water every day. Tofu should keep this way for about a week. Souring tofu will smell or taste sour, and may feel somewhat slippery to the touch.

Tofu Packed in Water in Plastic Tubs
Generally, tofu is sold this way in health and natural food stores, grocery stores and supermarkets. Stored in its original package, tofu will keep from a week to ten days. Look for the date stamped on the package in order to ascertain its freshness. Once you open the tub, the water should be changed every day and the tofu eaten within a week.

Vacuum-packaged Tofu
This is a form of packaging that will keep tofu fresh for three weeks to a month. Again, once the package is opened, the tofu should be stored in fresh water and used within a week to ten days.

The fresher the tofu, the fuller the flavor. Tofu begins to lose some of its subtle sweetness several days after being submerged in water. Generally, unless you plan to freeze it, buy or make only as much tofu as you think you will eat within a week (this can be longer with vacuum-packaged tofu). However, if you find that you have more tofu than you will be able to use within a week, one way to keep this surplus tofu fresh is to freeze it.

Frozen Tofu
Freezing will help retain not only tofu's freshness, but also its nutritional value. In fact, because it has lost most of its original water content, frozen tofu that has been thawed and squeezed has a higher proportion of protein to volume.

Tofu changes from the regular almost luminous or soft creamy white of unfrozen tofu to amber while frozen and then to a soft beige when thawed. Frozen tofu has a chewier and more porous, almost sponge-like texture, making it highly absorbent.

Although tofu in water-packed plastic tubs or vacuum packages may be frozen in its packages, the less water in the tofu, the finer the texture will be when thawed. You may wish to remove the tofu from these packages, then press or, at least, drain it, before freezing it.

Tofu will freeze faster if you cut the cakes into halves or thirds and press it. Wrap the slices well in plastic wrap or freezer paper, then seal in plastic bags or aluminum foil. It should be frozen for at least twelve hours for a satisfactory texture; freezing for two days to a week is even better.

You may also wish to try pressing tofu, then submerging it in a marinade and freezing the tofu in the marinade. Experimenting with these different possibilities will help you discover which texture you prefer or when one may be more appropriate than another in your own recipes.

To thaw frozen tofu, put it in a pan, cover it with boiling water, and let it stand for 10 to 15 minutes. If you have frozen whole cakes, cut the cakes in half after they begin to thaw slightly, so that they will defrost more quickly.

If the tofu has been frozen in a plastic tub or vacuum package, immerse it in very hot tap water for a few minutes until you can remove it from its package. Put the tofu in a pan, pour boiling water over it, and let it stand as described above.

When it has thawed, pour off the water, and add fresh cold water to rinse the tofu. Take the unfrozen cakes out of the water and press them gently between the palms of your hands to remove more water.

If you are going to crumble the defrosted tofu, or do not need the cakes or slices whole, you can wrap the tofu in a towel and squeeze out even more water. Tofu that has been frozen, then thawed and squeezed, will be even drier than drained and squeezed regular tofu. When fried, this crumbled frozen tofu browns nicely and has a texture remarkably similar to ground beef.

Frozen tofu's highly absorbent quality is useful in dishes which require marinating or cooking in sauces or broths. Its chewy texture makes it often more attractive to meat eaters than regular tofu, and it is nearly as versatile. What is more, because it thaws so quickly, it is convenient when you haven't got time to prepare something more elaborate.

Note: When a weight is given for the amount of frozen tofu required in a recipe, it refers to the tofu's pre-frozen weight.

Ways to Prepare Tofu

There are six simple techniques for preparing tofu that will take you through every recipe in this book. Parboiling, draining, pressing and squeezing are techniques that will firm tofu to varying degrees. Firming is generally done to reduce tofu's 80 to 85% water content so that it will hold together during more rigorous kinds of preparation and cooking, and to make the tofu more absorbent, so that it can more readily take on flavors from marinades, sauces and broths.

1 **Parboiling**
   Purpose: Parboiling will firm tofu slightly and increase its absorbing ability, and it will heat tofu through before serving it with sauces. Parboiling will also sweeten tofu and help stop it from souring.

   Method: Bring 2 cups of water to a boil, then add ½ tsp. salt (this gives the tofu a firmer texture but is optional). Put an 8 to 12-oz. cake of tofu into the water. When the water returns to a boil, remove the pan from the heat, and let stand for 2 to 3 minutes. Then remove the tofu.

   Comments: Parboiled tofu should be used right away. It is not very suitable for blended recipes (use drained, pressed or squeezed tofu instead). When parboiling tofu to halt souring, you may wish to omit the salt.

2 **Draining**
   Purpose: Draining will give a fairly firm tofu with a minimum of effort. It will also help preserve the subtle flavors of fresh tofu which diminish when it sits in water.

   Method: (Quick Method – 10 to 30 minutes) Set tofu in a flat pan or on a plate. Slant the pan or plate so that the water can drain to one end. The tofu can be draining while you are working on other parts of a recipe or meal. You can also use a colander to drain tofu.

(Refrigerator Method) Put the tofu in a colander and the colander over a bowl. Cover and refrigerate for 1 to 12 hours, no longer.

Comments: Do not drain for longer than 12 hours. Drained tofu can be used in recipes calling for crumbled or mashed tofu; also for slicing and cubing for salads, etc.

3 Pressing

Purpose: Tofu will achieve varying degrees of firmness depending upon the length of time pressed and the heaviness of the pressing weight. Pressing is done when you want the structure of the slices or cubes to remain intact for sautéeing, broiling, baking, pan- or deep-frying, in salads and in soups.

Method: Slice the cake of tofu into halves, thirds, or quarters, depending upon the thickness called for in a particular recipe. The slices should be of uniform thickness so that the tofu will press evenly. Put down one or two absorbent dish towels on a flat surface such as a cutting board or sturdy cookie sheet, and slant this surface. Spread the tofu slices on top of the towels and cover with one or two more dishtowels, making the top surface as flat as possible. Now put down another cutting board or sturdy cookie sheet − for even pressing − on top of the towels. Place a 2 to 5-lb. weight on top of that, and press for 20 minutes to an hour. For even firmer tofu, change towels every 10 minutes or so and use a 5-lb. weight.

Comments: A slice of well-pressed tofu will not fall apart when held up in the air by one corner. More care must be taken when pressing very soft or silken tofu. It is best to press these varieties of tofu very gently in whole cakes or sliced in half.

4 Squeezing

Purpose: Squeeze tofu after parboiling, draining or pressing to achieve a consistency similar to cottage cheese. You can also simply squeeze tofu to be used in blended dishes or in mashed or crumbled form where a reduced moisture content is desirable, but retaining the shape is not necessary.

Method: If desired, drain, press, or parboil a cake of tofu before squeezing, then put it into the center of a dishtowel, or use a tofu pressing sack. Twist the towel or sack closed, and squeeze or knead the tofu for 2 to 3 minutes, taking care not to press so vigorously that the tofu begins to come through. Empty into a bowl and use as desired.

Comments: Use for thicker dips, spreads, and puddings. Tofu that is squeezed, then crumbled and scrambled or fried, will brown well.

Other Preparatory and Cooking Techniques

5 Blending or Creaming

Blending is often required in recipes for dips, spreads, soups, sauces, dressings, puddings and pies.

If preparing a recipe in which only a small amount of liquid is to be blended with tofu, pour the liquid into the blender jar first. Slowly add the tofu, a bit at a time, so as not to overwork the blender.

A food processor is excellent for use when you must blend tofu to a cream without the use of any other liquid ingredients.

If the tofu must be blended with quite a bit of liquid, you will obtain a creamier mix if you add a small amount of the liquid first. Then proceed to add the tofu gradually as described above. Should the mixture become too thick, add a bit more liquid. When you have blended all the tofu, then add the remainder of the liquid gradually, keeping the blender on as you do so.

Draining, pressing or squeezing tofu before blending not only will give you a thicker mixture, but will also increase the absorbing ability of the tofu. Blended preparations develop a fuller taste if they have a few hours to sit or be chilled before serving so that the flavors can combine.

Putting whole cloves of garlic or whole onions into a food processor to be chopped tends to bring a bitter taste to the mixture blended with them. This does not seem to happen if the onions are sliced and the garlic is pressed beforehand.

6 Deep-frying

Basic Ingredients:

Oil: Use vegetable oil for light, crisp textures. Oils such as cottonseed and soy are satisfactory, especially when 10 to 30% sesame oil has been added for more flavor. The favorite oil among many Japanese is rapeseed oil, but it is not commonly available here.

Deep-frying oil can be re-used. When not using it for deep-frying, add some to other cooking for flavor and to help use it up. If you intend to save the deep-frying oil, allow the oil to cool fully, then pour it through a strainer into a glass jar. Close tightly, and store in a cool, dark place. When used oil becomes dark and thick, it should be discarded, as it will not yield crisp and light deep-fried foods and will produce off flavors.

When pouring used oil into the deep-frying pan, do so carefully without disturbing the sediment that may have collected in the bottom of the jar.

Always mix one part new oil with one part used oil.

When heating up the oil, do so gradually in order to get rid of any moisture that may be in the oil. Keep the temperature between 350° and 375°.

Batters: When deep-frying tofu, it isn't necessary to use a batter. If you do, one thing to remember is that the simpler and less rich the batter, the lighter and crisper the food will be. Rich batters absorb more oil.

Here are some suggestions for batter ingredients that you may wish to try:

1) dust with arrowroot, cornstarch or kudzu
2) coat with bread crumbs, flour or cornmeal
3) dust with flour or arrowroot, then dip in lightly beaten egg
4) dust with flour, dip in lightly beaten egg, then coat with bread crumbs
5) coat with tempura batter (p. 172)

Equipment: Your deep-frying pan can be a wok, a heavy 3- to 4-quart deep-frying pot, or an electric deep-fryer.

Another important piece of equipment is a deep-frying thermometer. It takes quite a bit of experience before most of us are able to tell when the oil is at the right temperature without the help of a thermometer. Be sure to use only a deep-frying thermometer. When testing the temperature of the oil, it is a good idea to warm up the thermometer by setting it in hot water; however, *before you immerse it in the oil, be sure to wipe it very dry, to avoid being spattered with hot oil.*

Other pieces of equipment which will make deep-frying easier are tongs or cooking chopsticks, a wire-mesh skimmer, and a draining rack.

Safety Precautions:

1) Keep handles of deep-frying pots turned inward so that there is less danger of the pot being accidentally knocked off the stove.

2) Have baking soda nearby in case of fire. Do not attempt to put out a fire by using water. This will only cause the fire to spread.

Method:

1) Fill the wok, deep-frying pan, or electric deep-fryer with oil to a level of 1½ to 2 inches. When deep-frying, it is a good idea not to fill any pan you are using more than half full of oil.

2) Heat up the oil to a temperature between 350° and 375°. If the temperature falls below 350°, the foods will be greasy. Above 375°, the oil will be damaged (unless you are using coconut oil which has a higher smoking point) and will produce off flavors.

3) Do not try to cook too many pieces of food at once, as this will lower the temperature of the oil too much, producing greasy food. It is best to deep-fry food of uniform size together, so that cooking times for food in one batch can be the same.

4) Pieces that are to be deep-fried should be at room temperature. Pat foods dry before putting into oil. Then, if uncoated, let them slide down the side of the pan or wok, or immerse them using tongs, chopsticks or a wire-mesh skimmer. It's a good idea to immerse these utensils in hot oil first so that the food will not stick to them when put into the oil.

5) After foods have cooked to a golden brown, remove them with tongs, chopsticks, or wire-mesh skimmer, and allow them to drain on a wire rack for several minutes. Then remove to paper toweling for 2 or 3 minutes more.

6) Before frying another batch, be sure that the oil has returned to the proper temperature.

7) Clean the oil with a skimmer every two or three batches. If you are using a batter that is especially crumbly, then clean the oil after every batch. The small pieces of cooked batter can be drained and reserved for use in salads, soups, etc. If storing these pieces, keep them refrigerated.

8) When finished, allow the deep-frying oil to cool *completely* before transferring it to a clean jar, if it is to be re-used.

To remove excess oil from deep-fried tofu to make it more absorbent for use in sauces, casseroles and soups, and make it even lighter and more easily digestible, try "dousing." This technique is especially recommended for people on low-fat diets, and can be used with pan-fried and sautéed foods as well.

Bring a quart of water to boil in a saucepan. Put the deep-fried food into a strainer or colander, or hold each piece between tongs or chopsticks. (Do not cut the tofu or other deep-fried foods before dousing.) Douse or immerse the tofu quickly in the boiling water. Drain for 1 minute, and then serve. Dousing can also be used to heat up deep-fried food.

Broiling after deep-frying also removes some surface oil. Do not douse before broiling. Broiling will brown the tofu nicely and give it a pleasant aroma. It can be done in an oven broiler, on an outside grill, or even in the toaster. Deep-frying tofu, like parboiling, is used to sweeten up souring tofu.

There are many uses for deep-fried tofu. After cooking, try thinly slicing deep-fried tofu cutlets (p. 166) for use in salads, soups, or casseroles. Or simmer whole cutlets, triangles, or cubes in sauces, broths or stews. Take care not to simmer too long because the tofu's texture will become increasingly porous and slightly tough. Try deep-fried tofu cubes in sandwiches, with eggs for breakfast, or use deep-fried tofu cubes with fondue. Frozen tofu can be deep fried as well.

Regular or medium-firm tofu should be well pressed before deep-frying so that it holds together while cooking. Be sure to pat dry before deep-frying.

Deep-fat frying should be done at the last minute before a meal. If you have a great deal of food to deep-fry, after cooking and draining each batch, put into a 250° oven to keep warm.

For recipes calling for deep-frying, see *Index*.

The Recipes

Points to Remember

1) The most commonly found tofu, Japanese-style regular, or medium firm, is the variety used in the recipes in this book. However, the Chinese-style firm tofu (see *Glossary*) may also be used. It can even be a time-saver in recipes calling for pressed tofu, since it is compact enough not to require pressing.

2) Japanese-style regular or medium-firm tofu is sold in several standard sizes, the most common being 8 oz., 12 oz., and 16 oz. An 8-oz. cake will measure *approximately* 4 × 4 × 1½ inches. An 8-oz. cake, mashed, will make approximately 1 to 1¼ cups. The more compact Chinese-style firm tofu is usually sold in 6-oz. cakes about ¾ to 1 inch thick. The weight will be given on the labels of pre-packaged tofu.

3) Although salt has been used in the recipes in this book, we have found that in most cases it may be left out without seriously affecting the overall taste. You may wish to compensate by adding or increasing other seasonings. Tofu itself is a low-sodium food.

4) The recipes are loosely arranged according to preparation and cooking time – from the quickest to the more involved.

5) The *Index* is arranged by main ingredients as well as by recipe names. For example, if you have potatoes on hand, check the *Index* under potato to find recipes in which they are the main ingredient.

6) Substitutions for special ingredients are given on p. 199.

Dips, Spreads and Appetizers

This section spans a whole range of dishes which might be served as hors d'oeuvres, made into canapés for a cocktail party, or featured as appetizers at a dinner. Some can be served as snacks or light entrées.

When preparing the dips and some of the uncooked spreads, we have found that those made with fresh flavorings, such as dill, basil, garlic and onion, are best eaten the day they are prepared. Fresh garlic and onion especially have a tendency to become bitter after the first day.

If you wish to make a dip or spread to have on hand for several days, it is best to use dried vegetable powders and herbs. If you are using very fresh dried herbs, substitute ⅓ tsp. of powdered herbs and ½ tsp. of crushed herbs for 1 Tbsp. of chopped fresh herbs. You may need to substitute more than 1 tsp. of dried crushed herbs for each Tbsp. of fresh herbs if the dried herbs are less fresh. For one clove of garlic, substitute between ⅛ and ¼ tsp. of garlic powder. Onion powder or minced onion can be substituted for fresh onion to taste.

If you prefer a heartier or thicker dip or spread, try substituting firm tofu (p. 204), or squeezed regular tofu (p. 22) before blending or processing. Use 75% of the amount of regular tofu called for, or, for example, 12 oz. of firm tofu for 16 oz. of regular tofu. If regular tofu is used, some water may collect on the top of the spread. This can be poured off or stirred back in, if you prefer the lighter consistency.

There are also recipes in other sections which could be easily adapted as hors d'oeuvres or appetizers. Bite-sized quiche tartlets could be made instead of Quiche Tarts (p. 156). Or you might try serving Beer Batter Nuggets (p. 174). Sauerkraut Balls in Mustard Sauce (p. 153) in a chafing dish is also a popular choice, especially for cold winter evenings.

One of our favorite easy-to-prepare appetizers are Deep-fried Tofu Cutlet Strips (p. 166) using regular or frozen tofu. They may be marinated first, or served with your favorite dipping sauce, or simply with Dijon or Kosciusko mustards.

These are just some suggestions. You will find plenty of new and different ones on your own.

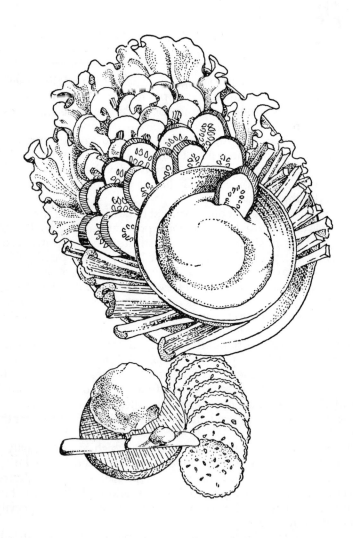

Curry Dip

This dip is especially well-suited for serving with fresh vegetables.

¼ cup oil, preferably safflower	Combine all ingredients, except tofu, in a blender.
2 Tbsp. lemon juice	
2 Tbsp. tomato catsup	Break or cut the tofu into small pieces. With the blender on, add it piece by piece, until all is blended and the mixture is very smooth. If you are using a food processor, break the tofu into small pieces, and blend briefly. Then add all other ingredients, and process until very smooth.
½ tsp. Worcestershire sauce	
½ tsp. curry powder	
½ tsp. dry mustard	
¼ tsp. garlic powder	
¼ tsp. salt	
8 oz. tofu	
Yield: 1½ cups.	

Horseradish Olive Dip

My mother created this recipe, and it is one of my favorite dips with potato chips. Try serving it also as a condiment the next time you cook beets.

8 oz. tofu, squeezed or pressed	Combine all ingredients, except the olives, in a food processor or blender and blend until smooth. (Since there is little liquid in this dip, adding the tofu a bit at a time will decrease the possibility of overworking your blender. The ingredients can also be mixed together with an electric beater, although the dip's consistency will not be as smooth.)
2 to 3 Tbsp. horseradish	
2 Tbsp. white wine vinegar	
2 Tbsp. chives	
1 tsp. olive oil	
¼ tsp. salt	
dash cayenne pepper	
¼ cup chopped ripe black olives (optional)	
	Stir in the chopped olives and transfer the dip to a serving bowl. Serve immediately or chill for a couple of hours to allow the flavors to blend more
Yield: 1¼ cups.	thoroughly.

Spinach Dip

This dip is excellent served with raw vegetables, especially sweet red peppers.

10 oz. fresh spinach	Wash the spinach carefully, and remove any stems and leaves that may be beginning to go bad.
12 oz. tofu	
3 Tbsp. lemon juice	
2 Tbsp. olive oil	Combine all the ingredients in a food processor or blender, and blend until smooth. If you are using a blender, you may wish to combine all ingredients, except the spinach and tofu, first. Then gradually blend in the spinach. After the spinach is completely mixed in, break up the tofu, and add it gradually until the mixture is smooth.
2 small cloves garlic, minced	
1²/₃ tsp. oregano	
1¹/₂ tsp. salt	
¹/₈ tsp. pepper	
Yield: approximately 3 cups.	

Dill Dip

This dip is wonderful when made with fresh dill and parsley, but it should be eaten the day it is made. Otherwise, use dried dill weed and parsley which keep better.

¹/₄ cup fresh dill, finely chopped (or 1 Tbsp. dried dill weed)	In a blender, combine all ingredients, except the tofu. Blend very well so that the dill and parsley will be very finely chopped.
2 Tbsp. fresh parsley, finely chopped (or 1 to 2 tsp. dried parsley)	
¹/₄ cup olive oil	Cut or break the tofu into small pieces, and add to the mixture in the blender, one piece at a time, until it is all blended and the dip is very smooth.
¹/₄ cup water	
3 Tbsp. lemon juice	
1 Tbsp. Worcestershire sauce	
1 tsp. vinegar	
1 tsp. soy sauce	
¹/₈ tsp. garlic powder	
¹/₂ tsp. liquid lecithin (optional)	
1 lb. tofu	
Yield: approximately 2 cups.	

Guacamole

3 Tbsp. lemon juice

¾ cup mashed tofu

1 Jalapeño pepper (optional)

3 to 4 ripe medium avocados

1 to 2 small tomatoes, very finely chopped

1 small onion, very finely chopped (or ½ tsp. onion powder)

1½ to 2 tsp. finely chopped green chili peppers

½ tsp. salt

⅛ tsp. garlic powder

Yield: 2 to 2½ cups.

Pour the lemon juice into a blender. Add the mashed tofu, bit by bit, and blend until smooth. If you wish to use the Jalapeño pepper in the guacamole, chop one pepper very finely, then add it to the tofu-lemon mixture, and blend thoroughly.

Mash the avocados in a bowl. Add the tofu mixture and all other ingredients, and combine thoroughly.

The guacamole can be served immediately or chilled, but it is best eaten the day it is made.

Quick Creamy Onion Dip

½ cup light oil (salad or olive oil)

½ cup water

3 Tbsp. lemon juice

1 Tbsp. wine vinegar

1¾ lb. tofu

1 envelope Liptons Onion Recipe and Soup Mix or any natural dehydrated onion soup mix

Yield: 3 cups.

Combine the liquid ingredients in a blender. Break or cut tofu into small pieces, and with the blender on, add the tofu, piece by piece, until it is all blended, and the mixture is very smooth.

Turn into a bowl, and mix in the onion soup mix. Refrigerate for at least 30 minutes before serving.

Mushroom Dip

2 cups fresh mushrooms, finely chopped	Sauté the chopped mushrooms in the butter or soy margarine until soft. Then add the chopped scallions, and sauté for one more minute.
4 Tbsp. butter or soy margarine	
3 scallions, chopped	
1 to 1½ cups mashed tofu	Mix together the mashed tofu, lemon juice, soy sauce, thyme and salt.
1 to 2 tsp. lemon juice	
2 tsp. natural soy sauce or tamari	Add the sautéed mushrooms and scallions to this mixture, and mix well.
¼ tsp. thyme	Adjust seasonings, if necessary.
pinch of salt	
Yield: 2½ cups.	

Basiga Dip

3 Tbsp. olive oil	Blend all ingredients until smooth, adding the tofu gradually to the other ingredients.
1 to 3 cloves garlic (or ¼ to ½ tsp. garlic powder*)	
2 tsp. lemon juice	Allow several hours for flavors to meld before serving.
1 Tbsp. fresh basil (or ¾ tsp. dried basil)	Note: Three cloves of garlic, unless you happen to have freshly harvested garlic, is a large amount even for people who generally consider themselves inveterate garlic eaters. Start with one, then taste. Add more if you like.
½ to 1 tsp. salt	
8 oz. tofu	
Yield: approximately 1½ cups.	

*Since most commercially pre-packaged garlic powder found in supermarkets and grocery stores contains chemicals, additives and/or colorings of one kind or another, you may wish to purchase your garlic powder from food co-operatives or health food stores. The leading supplier to these sources, Gilroy Foods Inc., has confirmed that their Premium and Special Garlic Powders contain no chemicals, additives or colorings.

Black Bean Dip

This is what my friend Martha's aunt would call a "candlelight dish." It tastes good, but its appearance requires colorful garnishes, like fresh parsley, sieved egg yolks or chopped scallions.

1½ cups cooked black beans
3 Tbsp. lemon juice
2 Tbsp. olive oil
2 tsp. cumin
1 to 1½ tsp. salt
8 oz. tofu
chopped scallions, as garnish

Yield: approximately 2 cups.

In a food processor or blender, blend all ingredients, except the chopped scallions, until creamy smooth, adding the tofu gradually to the other ingredients.

Garnish with chopped scallions, and serve.

Note: ¾ cup of dry black beans soaked overnight and then cooked in 3 cups of water will yield approximately 1½ cups of cooked beans. Cooking time should be about 1½ hours.

Deviled Tofu

Taste the resemblance to egg salad, and enjoy the lightness and much lower cholesterol content, especially if you use Tofu Mayonnaise. This dish can be served as a dip or sandwich spread.

1 lb. tofu
¼ to ½ cup mayonnaise, or Tofu Mayonnaise (p. 97)
¼ tsp. coriander
⅛ tsp. cumin
½ tsp. curry powder
¼ tsp. salt
⅛ tsp. paprika
dash garlic powder
¼ tsp. natural soy sauce or tamari
1 Tbsp. Dijon mustard
¼ cup pickle relish
¼ cup celery, diced

Yield: approximately 3 cups.

Press or squeeze the tofu for half an hour (p. 22). Mash it, and add all the remaining ingredients. Mix well.

Tofu Hummus

⅓ cup sesame seeds
⅓ cup fresh lemon juice
8 oz. tofu
⅓ cup tahini
½ to 1 tsp. salt
3 to 4 medium cloves garlic
16-oz. can garbanzo beans, or 1¼ cups cooked garbanzo beans
chopped parsley, as garnish

Toast the sesame seeds in a heavy pan over low to medium heat until they begin to pop. Move the pan back and forth or stir gently to prevent the seeds from sticking to the bottom of the pan.

Place the toasted seeds in a blender, and grind them at high speed. Add the lemon juice, and blend for 1 minute.

Place all other ingredients, except the parsley, in a food processor or mixing bowl. Add the lemon juice mixture. Blend together for 1 to 2 minutes until the mixture has a smooth, soft texture. If you prefer not to blend the garbanzo beans so thoroughly, add them during the last 20 to 30 seconds of processing or blending.

People have very strong feelings about how hummus should be seasoned. Some prefer a more prominent taste of lemon juice, others prefer more tahini, and still others want a very strong garlic flavor. At this point taste the hummus, and adjust the seasonings as you prefer.

Chill, and serve garnished with chopped parsley.

Yield: approximately 3½ cups.

Savory Cheese Spread

Are you often in need of a hot appetizer that can be prepared quickly? Try this one.

½ cup grated Cheddar cheese
½ cup grated Parmesan cheese
½ cup mashed tofu
½ cup mayonnaise, or Tofu Mayonnaise (p. 97)
¼ cup diced green olives
2 Tbsp. grated onion
2 Tbsp. chopped chives or parsley
1 tsp. curry powder
French bread
parsley, as garnish
Yield: 16 to 20 hors d'oeuvres.

Combine all ingredients except the bread. Toast slices of French bread, spread with cheese-tofu mixture and broil until cheese is melted. Garnish with small sprigs of parsley.

Tofu Miso Sandwich Spread

2 Tbsp. miso
1 Tbsp. oil
1 cup mashed tofu
1 carrot, finely grated (approx. ⅔ cup)
1 small onion, minced
¼ cup finely diced dill pickle
1 tsp. lemon juice
¼ tsp. garlic powder (optional)
Yield: approximately 2½ cups.

Mix the miso and oil together until smooth.

In a mixing bowl, combine the remaining ingredients. Stir in the miso-oil mixture, and mix well.

Serve with shredded lettuce in pita bread or with lightly flavored crackers such as stoned wheat thins or thin rice crackers.

Spinach Vegetable Spread

6 Tbsp. lemon juice
2 Tbsp. light vegetable or salad oil (preferably olive)
1 lb. tofu, pressed or squeezed (p. 22)
6 Tbsp. dehydrated vegetable flakes
1 Tbsp. chives
½ tsp. salt
¼ to ½ tsp. garlic powder, to taste
¼ to ½ tsp. onion powder, to taste
¼ tsp. cumin
⅛ tsp. turmeric
dash cayenne pepper
dash black pepper
10 oz. fresh spinach, washed with stems removed

If you are using a food processor, combine all ingredients, except the spinach, and blend until smooth. If you are using a blender, first blend together the lemon juice and oil. Then add the tofu, bit by bit, and blend until smooth. It is also a good idea to crush the dehydrated vegetable somewhat – using a mortar and pestle, for example – before adding them to the tofu mixture. The other seasonings may be added at the same time. Blend in well, then transfer to a 1½-quart bowl.

Before adding the spinach, be sure that it is as dry as possible. You may wish to squeeze it in absorbent cloth or paper toweling. Chop the spinach and add it to the mixture in the bowl. This will be easier if you stir in the spinach a bit at a time.

Chill the spread for at least an hour to allow the dehydrated vegetables to soften.

Variations:
1. Use the same amount of tofu, oil, and lemon juice as above, but instead of unseasoned dehydrated vegetables and the seasonings, try a dehydrated vegetable soup mix, such as a 1⅝ oz. package of Knorr Vegetable Soupmix. Pour the contents of the mix into a measuring cup. Shake the cup so that the seasoning falls to the bottom of the cup. Remove the dehydrated vegetables and add them to the tofu mixture. Then add the seasonings left in the bottom of the measuring cup a bit at a time, testing after each addition. These soup mixes are often highly seasoned and quite salty, so test frequently to avoid over-seasoning.
2. Proceed as above but leave out the spinach. This may be used as a spread or as a dip with fresh vegetables or chips.

Yield: approximately 4 cups.

Miso Tahini Spread

In this recipe, at least half of the vegetables should be onion, and the rest, carrot or beet. Try this spread on toast with dill or sweet pickle.

2 to 3 Tbsp. miso
2 to 3 Tbsp. water
¼ to ½ cup finely minced vegetables (½ onion and ½ carrot or beet)
1 Tbsp. oil
1 cup tahini

Dissolve the miso in the water, and set aside. You may wish to use a blender for a smooth mixture.

Sauté the vegetables for 5 minutes in the oil. Fairly high heat can be used; the vegetables may be crisp.

Lower the heat, add the tahini, and stirring constantly, sauté until brown and fragrant. This will take from 5 to 10 minutes, depending to a great extent on the type of tahini you have. (Tahini will tend to stick to the bottom of the pan and take on a mealy rather than creamy texture.)

When the tahini is ready, remove from heat, and *immediately* add the miso-water mixture. Stir thoroughly at this point, or the oil will separate from the rest of the spread.

Serve warm or cool, but do not refrigerate as the spread will become hard and unworkable.

Yield: 1½ cups.

Tofu Raisin Nut Spread

1/2 cup pecans or walnuts
1/2 cup raisins
8 oz. tofu, pressed or squeezed (p. 22)
2 Tbsp. oil
2 Tbsp. honey
1 tsp. lemon juice
1 tsp. vanilla
1/4 tsp. cinnamon

Yield: 2 cups.

To toast the nuts, spread them out on a cookie sheet and put them into a 350° oven for 5 to 10 minutes, or until they darken in color and become fragrant. Then chop them finely.

Chop the raisins.

In a blender or food processor, purée the tofu with the oil.

Pour the puréed tofu into a bowl, and add all the remaining ingredients, mixing well.

Pineapple Cashew Spread

This is a sweet spread, well-suited for serving with Boston Brown Bread (p. 177). It is also delicious served on top of fresh fruit.

3/4 cup pineapple (canned or fresh), well drained
1/4 cup honey
3 1/2 tsp. lemon juice
1 tsp. vanilla
1/4 tsp. powdered ginger
1/8 tsp. salt
8 oz. tofu, pressed or squeezed
1/2 cup cashew nuts

Yield: approximately 2 1/2 cups.

Combine all the ingredients in a food processor or blender, and blend until smooth. If you are using a blender, you may wish to blend all ingredients, except the tofu and cashew nuts, first. Then break the tofu into smaller pieces, and while the blender is on, gradually add them to the mixture in the blender. The cashews can be added in the same way at the end.

Almond Mushroom Paté

As preparation goes very quickly once you begin sautéeing, it is a good idea to have all vegetables chopped beforehand and the necessary seasonings close at hand. This paté is very versatile. Try serving it in the suggested variations.

¾ cup blanched almonds
1 small onion, finely chopped
3 Tbsp. butter
4½ cups mushrooms, chopped
2 cloves garlic, minced
2 tsp. lemon juice
½ tsp. salt
⅓ tsp. dried tarragon
pinch of black pepper
¼ cup mashed tofu
tarragon or parsley sprigs as garnish
lemon wedges

Preheat oven to 325°. Toast the blanched almonds on a baking sheet, stirring occasionally, until golden, 10 to 15 minutes. Set aside to cool.

Using a large skillet, sauté the chopped onion in 1 Tbsp. of butter until golden, about 3 minutes. Add the remaining 2 Tbsp. of butter, the mushrooms, garlic, lemon juice, salt, tarragon, and pepper. Cook over high heat for 2 minutes, stirring constantly. Remove the vegetables with a slotted spoon and place in a bowl. Cook the pan juices over high heat until reduced to 1 Tbsp.

Process the toasted almonds in a blender or food processor until finely ground. Add the cooked vegetables, pan juices, and mashed tofu. Blend until almost smooth.

Spoon mixture into a 2-cup serving bowl, cover and refrigerate until chilled, 2 hours, or overnight.

Serve garnished with tarragon or parsley sprigs and lemon wedges, accompanied by lightly flavored crisp crackers.

Variations:
1. Use as a sandwich spread with a thin layer of cream cheese and alfalfa sprouts.

2. Prepare filo dough as you would for Tiropites (p. 48). (You will need 1 lb. of dough.) Use this paté for the filling, and serve with sour cream.

Yield: 2 cups.

Walnut Spinach Tofu Paté

This paté is a popular choice among customers at Toronto's Soja Soyfood Café and Delicatessen. Slices of it are served with thin wheat or rye crackers, colorful fresh vegetables, Soja's own Tofu Mayonnaise (p. 97) and French mustard. It may also be packed into a bowl, with sprigs of fresh parsley, and served as a spread.

1½ cups finely chopped onion
3 Tbsp. oil
1½ Tbsp. sherry or sake
10-oz. spinach, washed and dried
8 oz. walnuts
1¼ lb. tofu
¼ cup and 2 Tbsp. miso
1 Tbsp. Dijon mustard
½ tsp. thyme
½ tsp. rosemary
½ tsp. sage

Yield: 1 loaf.

Preheat the oven to 375°.

Sauté the onion in the oil until translucent. Add the sherry or sake, and cook until the liquid is reduced by half. Be careful not to scorch the onions.

Mince the spinach very, very finely. This must be done by hand; a food processor will not do a proper job.

Grind the walnuts to crumb-size in a food processor or blender. Add to the spinach. Add onion-sake mixture.

Process the tofu bit by bit until smooth, then add the miso, mustard, and herbs. Add this to the spinach mixture, and combine well.

Line a loaf pan (8½″ × 4½″ × 2½″) with brown paper that has been thoroughly saturated with oil. Put in the paté mixture, then knock the bottom of the pan against a table or countertop to get rid of all air bubbles. Fold the oiled brown paper loosely over the paté mixture. Cover with a double layer of aluminum foil, poking a few holes in the foil to allow steam to escape during cooking.

Place the loaf pan in a large pan or dish and then fill the dish with 2 inches of water. Bake in the oven for 1½ to 2 hours, then remove the pan with water, and bake the paté alone for ½ hour.

Zucchini Rounds

Although these are delightful appetizers, we often eat them as a main dish on warm summer evenings.

3 medium zucchini
8 oz. tofu
1/4 cup chopped green onion
6 Tbsp. Parmesan cheese
1/2 tsp. basil
1/2 tsp. salt
1/4 tsp. garlic powder
1/2 cup bread crumbs, as topping

Yield: 6 to 8 servings as an appetizer.

Cut the zucchini into 3/4-inch thick slices, and lightly steam for 5 to 7 minutes.

Meanwhile, thoroughly blend the tofu bit by bit in a food processor. (If you use a blender instead, you may have to add a little water or soymilk. Add as little as possible, a scant Tbsp. at a time.) As soon as the tofu is very smooth, turn into a mixing bowl.

Add all the other filling ingredients to the tofu in the mixing bowl, and mix.

After the steamed zucchini has cooled slightly, carefully remove one half of the inside pulp from each slice, leaving the bottom and outer skin intact.

Mash the zucchini pulp, and add it to the filling ingredients. Mix well.

Spoon filling back into the zucchini rounds, heaping them full.

Set the rounds on a 9 × 12-inch cookie sheet. Sprinkle with bread crumbs, and broil for 3 to 6 minutes, until crispy on top.

Serve warm.

Soja's Rice Age Stuffing

Age (AH-gay) is the Japanese word for deep-fried tofu pouch (see Glossary). Deep-fried tofu pouches are not yet widely available here, although some Japanese grocery stores do carry them under the Japanese name.

You can make very satisfactory pouches out of deep-fried tofu cutlets (p. 166). This is the stuffing which Soja, Toronto's tofu restaurant, uses in its tofu pouches. They make a delightful appetizer or light meal.

2 to 4 Tbsp. oil
¼ cup sunflower seeds
3 green onions, thinly sliced
¼ cup finely chopped celery
3 Tbsp. finely chopped green pepper
¾ cup grated carrots
1½ tsp. grated ginger root
¼ cup chopped fresh parsley
2½ to 3 cups cooked brown rice
3 Tbsp. natural soy sauce or tamari
8 deep-fried tofu pouches

Yield: stuffing for approximately 16 half pouches.

If you are preparing deep-fried tofu pouches from tofu cutlets, see pp. 166 to 167 for instructions.

To prepare the stuffing, heat the oil in a skillet or wok, and sauté the sunflower seeds until brown, then remove with a slotted spoon. In the remaining oil stir-fry the green onion for 1 minute. Add the celery, green pepper and carrots, and fry for 1 minute more. Then add the grated ginger, parsley, and cooked rice. When the rice has been heated through, add the soy sauce or tamari.

To stuff, cut 8 deep-fried tofu pouches in half, spread apart, and put ¼ to ⅓ cup of stuffing into each half-pouch. Serve warm or chilled.

Stuffed Mushrooms

24 large, fresh mushrooms
1 small onion, finely chopped
3 cloves garlic, pressed
3 Tbsp. butter
1/2 tsp. thyme
1/4 tsp. salt
12 oz. frozen tofu (p. 19), thawed and finely chopped
1/2 cup bread crumbs
1 tsp. Worcestershire sauce
1/4 cup white wine
1/4 cup grated mild Cheddar cheese
2 Tbsp. fresh parsley, finely chopped

Yield: 8 to 10 servings as an appetizer.

Preheat oven to 375°.

Remove the stems from the mushrooms, and reserve. With a small rounded spoon or a melon baller, gently scoop out the insides of the mushroom caps. There is no need to dig deeply. Put what you scoop out into a 2-cup measuring cup.

Finely chop your reserved stems, and add them to the measuring cup until you have 1½ cups of chopped mushroom pieces.

Sauté the chopped onions and pressed garlic in 2 Tbsp. of butter until clear and translucent. Then add the mushroom pieces, thyme, and salt.

Cook 2 to 3 minutes.

Add the tofu, bread crumbs, and Worcestershire sauce to the onion-mushroom mix, and cook for 3 to 4 minutes more to blend flavors.

Meanwhile sauté the mushroom caps very gently in 1 Tbsp. of butter to partially cook them. Cook 2 minutes on each side, then remove from heat.

After the onion-mushroom-tofu mix has finished cooking, remove from heat and add the wine. Toss gently to mix the wine throughout. Add the grated cheese and chopped parsley and mix again.

Mound the stuffing into the mushroom caps, and place in a well-oiled pan or baking dish. Bake for 15 minutes.

Tiropites

These delightful little turnovers made with flaky Greek filo dough can be served as appetizers or as a light entrée with tossed salad. For a large group of people we use a pound of filo dough and fill the first half pound of dough with the filling below. The second half pound we often fill with Almond Mushroom Paté (p. 43). Even very skeptical teenagers who often ask "Does this have 'toad food' in it?" have been won over by these tiropites.

DOUGH:

8 oz. filo dough

olive oil or melted butter to brush filo leaves

FILLING:

8 oz. tofu

1 egg

1 Tbsp. oregano

1½ to 2 tsp. salt

³⁄₈ tsp. pepper

Yield: 4 to 6 servings as an appetizer.

Preheat oven to 350°.

To prepare the filo dough, lay one leaf of it down on a damp cloth. Brush with olive oil or melted butter using a soft pastry brush. Lay the next leaf of filo on top of it, and again brush with olive oil. Continue stacking and coating the leaves in this manner until you have used 8 oz. of filo.

Cut the stack of leaves into 3-inch squares. (Generally we are able to get approximately 18 squares from the brand of filo dough which we buy.) While you prepare the filling keep the dough covered with a damp cloth.

Now to the filling. Mash the tofu, and then mix in the egg, oregano, salt and pepper.

Divide the filling equally among the squares. If you have 18 squares, this will come to approximately 1 Tbsp. per square. Fold over each square of leaves to make small turnovers. Moisten the edges of each turnover with water, and press firmly to seal. Brush the tops with olive oil or melted butter.

Place the turnovers on a lightly oiled or buttered cookie sheet, and bake for 30 to 35 minutes until they are puffed and golden.

Serve hot.

Nori-Wrapped Hors d'oeuvres

These are simple and very elegant in appearance, and are a good way to introduce yourself and others to the very nutritious and delicious sea vegetable, nori *or* laver *(see Glossary).*

1 to 1¼ lb. (2 cakes) tofu, pressed firmly
2 cloves garlic, pressed
2 Tbsp. oil
dash hot pepper sauce (optional)
4 sheets nori

DIPPING SAUCE:

3 Tbsp. natural soy sauce or tamari
3 Tbsp. water
1 Tbsp. lemon juice
1 Tbsp. rice wine vinegar*
¼ heaping tsp. dry mustard
2 Tbsp. minced onion
1 Tbsp. grated fresh ginger

*Instead of using 1 Tbsp. each of rice wine vinegar and lemon juice, you may wish to use 2 Tbsp. of either rice wine vinegar or lemon juice.

After you have firmly pressed the tofu, cut each cake into eight sticks.

In a large skillet, lightly sauté the pressed garlic. As soon as it starts to brown, add the tofu. Lower the heat, and cook gently, turning the tofu to brown on all sides. When turning the tofu, be careful that it does not break.

When the tofu sticks are browned on all sides, before removing them from the heat, sprinkle hot sauce (scant ¼ tsp.) on them, if desired. Spread the sauce with the back of a spoon to distribute it more evenly over the surface of the tofu sticks.

Remove the tofu from the heat, and cool to room temperature. If the tofu sticks appear to be oily, set them to drain on paper toweling.

At this point the dipping sauce can be prepared. Combine the soy sauce, water, lemon juice, rice wine vinegar, and dry mustard. Mix well, and then add the minced onion and grated fresh ginger.

Toast the nori. This is done by holding a sheet 2 to 3 inches above low heat. The nori will lighten in color as you toast it.

After you have toasted the nori, stack the sheets on top of each other. Using a very sharp knife, cut the large sheets into quarters.

Now put down a tofu stick onto one of the small sheets of nori. If the nori is longer than the tofu stick, you may wish to cut off the excess nori. (If you have strips of leftover nori, try dipping it into the sauce. It's very tasty eaten alone, too.)

Roll one piece of nori around each stick of tofu as shown. Moisten the end of the nori with water so that it will stick, and set aside with the moistened overlap on the bottom.

After you have wrapped all the tofu sticks, cut them into quarters with your sharp knife.

Arrange these on a plate, and sprinkle with a few pieces of grated ginger. Tofu centers should be visible.

Yield: 64 nori-wrapped hors d'oeuvres; 8 to 10 servings.

Place tooth picks next to the serving plate, and serve with the dipping sauce.

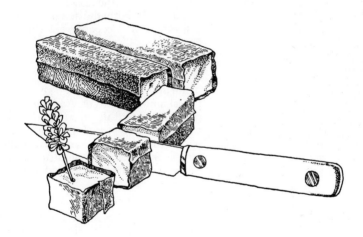

Baked Vegetable Rissole

A rissole is traditionally a deep-fried or baked pastry of French origin which is filled with finely ground and seasoned meat, poultry, or fish. This recipe makes use of East Indian seasonings and fresh snap peas.

PASTRY:

1½ cups flour

½ tsp. salt

½ cup butter or soy margarine

⅓ cup ice water

FILLING:

1 lb. tofu

1 medium onion, finely chopped

1 clove garlic, pressed

2 Tbsp. oil

¾ tsp. salt

½ tsp. cumin

⅛ tsp. nutmeg

⅛ tsp. turmeric

⅛ tsp. coriander

1½ cups thinly sliced fresh snap peas (including pods) or thawed frozen peas

To make the pastry, sift together the flour and salt. If you are using a salted soy margarine, you may wish to cut down on the salt, or eliminate it entirely.

Cut the margarine or butter into the dry ingredients using two knives, a pastry blender, or food processor until the mixture has the consistency of cornmeal. Then sprinkle in the ice water, and blend lightly. Form the dough into a ball, wrap it in wax paper, and chill for one hour.

Press or squeeze the tofu for 20 to 30 minutes (p. 22), then mash it.

Sauté the onion and pressed garlic in the oil until translucent. Add the mashed tofu and all other ingredients, except the snap peas. Turn with a spatula to coat the tofu and onions with the spices. Sauté for 3 to 4 minutes longer. Remove from the heat, immediately add the peas, and toss.

Preheat the oven to 400°.

When the dough is ready, roll it out until it is ⅛-inch thick, then cut twenty circles from 3½ to 4 inches in diameter. (Another way to prepare the dough is to divide it into 20 small balls, and then roll out circles of the above dimensions.)

Spoon 1½ to 2 Tbsp. of filling onto one side of each circle, then cover with the other half of the circle, making small turnovers. Seal tightly, decorating the edges if you wish. Prick the tops once with a fork.

Put the rissoles on cookie sheets, and bake for 10 to 12 minutes, or until brown.

Yield: 20 rissoles; 4 servings as a light entrée, or 6 as an appetizer.

Egg Rolls

The two egg roll recipes which follow are among our favorite recipes. One calls for the more traditional oriental ingredients: dried Chinese mushrooms, bok choy or Chinese cabbage, saifun or cellophane noodles, and richly flavorful and fragrant dark sesame oil. These ingredients can be purchased in oriental grocery and specialty food stores, or may be found in the oriental and gourmet food sections of large supermarkets.

The second recipe calls for frozen tofu (p. 19) and ingredients which are readily available in most grocery stores. Egg roll wrappers are an increasingly common sight in the frozen or refrigerated food sections of these stores.

Generally when we make egg rolls, we make some of each kind. Each recipe will make 12 egg rolls, and there are usually 24 egg roll wrappers in the packages we buy.

Egg rolls can be served as an appetizer or as a main dish. Serve them with fresh vegetables and dipping sauces (pp. 100 to 101) or the Mustard Sauce on p. 174. Try wrapping an egg roll in a fresh leaf of lettuce; it's easy to hold and delicious, too.

RECIPE #1: Oriental Style

½ package (or 12) egg roll wrappers

1 egg, beaten

oil for deep-frying

FILLING:

12 oz. tofu

5 large dried Chinese mushrooms

1 cup cellophane or saifun noodles

1 cup finely shredded bok choy or cabbage

¼ cup scallions, finely chopped

1 to 1½-inch piece fresh ginger root

3 Tbsp. vegetable oil

2 cloves garlic, pressed

1½ to 2 Tbsp. natural soy sauce or tamari

1½ Tbsp. dark sesame oil

⅛ tsp. hot pepper sauce (optional)

Press the tofu for 20 to 30 minutes, and then mash. Soak the mushrooms in 2 cups of water for 30 minutes. Soak saifun noodles for the same amount of time.

Peel a 1 to 1½-inch piece of ginger root, and slice it vertically into very thin pieces no thicker than 1/16 inch. Turn over these pieces on the cutting board, flat-side down, and cut them into matchstick pieces until you have 1½ Tbsp.

In a skillet or wok, heat the vegetable oil over medium heat. When the oil is hot, but not smoking, drop in the ginger and pressed garlic, and cook about 1 minute until lightly browned. Remove from oil with a wire-mesh strainer or slotted spoon, and drain on absorbent paper or toweling. The oil has now been flavored for the cooking of the other vegetables.

Remove the stems from the soaked mushrooms, discarding the tougher ones. Finely slice the mushrooms and remaining stems.

Sauté the mushrooms and stems for 5 to 10 minutes in the skillet or wok. Add the cabbage, and stir-fry for 2 to 3 minutes more. Then add the mashed tofu and soy sauce. Once this is done, remove the mixture from the heat.

Drain the noodles, then put on a cutting board, and cut into 2-inch lengths. Add the noodles, chopped scallions, and dark sesame oil to the other ingredients, and toss. If desired, sprinkle the hot pepper sauce into the mixture. Turn onto a large plate or platter, and set aside to cool.

Fold the egg rolls, as shown on the following page.

DEEP-FRYING THE EGG ROLLS:

1. Read the section on deep frying (pp. 23 to 26), if you haven't already.
2. Pour enough oil into a deep-fryer, wok, or deep-sided skillet so that you have at least 2 inches of oil in the pan.
3. Slowly heat the oil to 350°. Maintaining the temperature of the oil between 350° and 365° will prevent greasy egg rolls.
4. To keep the temperature within this range, do not cook too many egg rolls at one time. A deep-frying thermometer will tell you how many egg rolls can be added without lowering the temperature of the oil to below 350°.
5. Cook the egg rolls for 2 to 3 minutes, or until golden brown, then turn over and cook for 30 seconds to 1 minute again until golden brown. Lift out with cooking chopsticks, a wire-mesh strainer or a slotted spoon.
6. Drain on a wire rack, then on paper toweling.

Yield: 12 egg rolls.

Folding Egg Rolls

1. Place the egg roll wrapper so that it is a diamond shape. Put 3 Tbsp. of filling on it horizontally just below the mid-point.

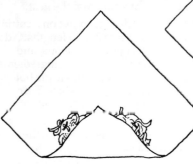

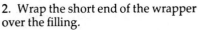

2. Wrap the short end of the wrapper over the filling.

3. Bring the right-hand point toward the center, taking care to tuck in the corner, so that the filling is not visible and will not fall out. Bring the left-hand point toward the center in the same manner.

4. Brush the tip of the unrolled portion of the wrapper with beaten egg.

5. Roll the egg roll toward the point which you have coated with the egg. Keep the uncooked egg rolls covered with a slightly damp cloth to prevent them from drying out.

RECIPE #2: Western Style

½ package (or 12)
egg roll wrappers

1 egg, beaten

oil for deep-frying

FILLING:

1¼ lb. frozen tofu (p. 19)

3 Tbsp. sesame oil

1 small onion, finely chopped

2 cloves garlic, pressed

1½ cups finely
chopped mushrooms

1 carrot, grated

2 cups finely shredded cabbage

1 Tbsp. natural soy sauce
or tamari

1 rounded tsp. powdered ginger

½ tsp. salt

dash of black pepper

1 Tbsp. wine vinegar

Yield: 12 egg rolls.

Thaw frozen tofu, and chop finely.

Heat sesame oil over medium high heat, but do not allow it to smoke, and sauté the vegetables, adding them in the following order: 1) chopped onion and pressed garlic; cook for ½ minute, then add 2) finely chopped mushrooms; cook for 1 minute, then add 3) grated carrot; cook for ½ to 1 minute, then add 4) finely shredded cabbage; cook for ½ to 1 minute.

Immediately after adding the cabbage, add the soy sauce, ginger, salt, and pepper. Remove from heat, and add the chopped tofu. Mix well.

Add the vinegar, tossing lightly, and turn out onto a large plate or platter to cool.

For wrapping and deep-frying, follow the instructions given in the preceding recipe.

Variation:
Try serving this filling with Tofu Mayonnaise (p. 97) and shredded lettuce on pita bread. It makes a light but satisfying sandwich.

Soups

Perhaps the most important point that should be stressed at the beginning of this section is that when preparing soups with a soymilk base, one must be careful not to boil the soymilk. This is especially true when ingredients such as wine, soy sauce, Worcestershire sauce, lemon juice or salt have been added. When boiled, soymilk will begin to curdle. This also happens to dairy milk if it is boiled with certain ingredients such as wine, although dairy milk is slightly more stable.

The soups will not have to be thrown out if you boil the soymilk. They will be quite tasty, but their consistency will not be as light and creamy as they should be (they will be like a soft custard). Soymilk-based soups can be very delicate, and will taste best if the soymilk is kept just below scalding while preparing the soup.

Soymilk can be bought bottled in soyfoods delicatessens, health or natural food stores, and some supermarkets. There are also a number of soymilk powders on the market. If you do not have soymilk, dairy milk can be substituted.

After reading through the recipes in this section, you may wish to try adding tofu to your favorite soup recipes. Deep-fried tofu cubes (p. 167) or crumbled frozen tofu (p. 19) absorb flavors very well, and can add a tender, chewy texture to soups. Or try pressing tofu, then slicing it into thin, noodle-like strips and floating them in your favorite clear broth with an array of colorful vegetables. You will be giving these soups a significant protein boost with few additional calories, carbohydrates or fats. And you do not need to worry about tofu overwhelming the flavors of the original dish.

Miso Noodle Soup

We eat miso soup any time of day. It is especially good in the morning for breakfast, because of the energizing effect of the miso (see Glossary).

Miso soup enjoys a long tradition in Japan. It is a soup which may be made with nearly unlimited variations and is considered suitable for serving at any meal in any season.

The basic formula consists of two to three vegetables cooked in a stock to which generally 1 Tbsp. of miso is added for every serving. For children or those preferring a blander taste you can cut down the amount of miso to ½ to 1 tsp.

The recipe below is only one example of miso soup. You can experiment on your own with other vegetables and seasonings. This soup is a particular favorite of mine because the tofu "noodles" remind me so much of the noodles in Chicken Noodle Soup, a childhood favorite.

Ingredients	
4 cups vegetable stock or water	
1½ cups finely sliced mushrooms	
⅓ cup finely sliced onions	
¼ tsp. minced fresh ginger root (optional)	
4 oz. tofu	
4 Tbsp. miso (Hatcho, Barley or Brown Rice, or a combination)	

Bring the water or stock to a boil. Meanwhile slice the mushrooms and onions very finely and mince the ginger root. Slice the tofu into noodle-like strips, no wider or thicker than ¼ inch.

When the water or stock boils, add the mushrooms, onions, and ginger root. Bring to a boil, then simmer for 5 minutes. Add the tofu noodles during the last minute of cooking.

Remove from heat. Spoon 4 to 6 Tbsp. of soup broth into a small bowl or measuring cup. Then add the miso to the liquid and mash in until smooth. This can also be done in the blender, in which case you may wish to use more liquid. Pour the blended miso back into the soup and stir.

Yield: 4 servings.

Serve immediately.

Hot Miso Broth

This broth can be used as a soup base for your favorite ingredients, or you can drink it as is at any time of the day. Miso broth can give you energy that is calming, and at the same time, long lasting.

1 cup water or vegetable stock	Heat the water to boiling. Add the ginger root and boil for 1 minute. Remove from heat and let sit for 1 to 2 minutes. Then pour 2 to 3 Tbsp. of ginger water into a cup or bowl. Add the miso, and mash in until smooth. Pour back into the remaining ginger water, mix, and serve immediately.
1/2 tsp. grated ginger root (optional)	
1 Tbsp. miso (Hatcho, Barley or Brown Rice)	
Yield: 1 serving.	

Sauerkraut Soup

Try this soup on a cloudy, cold day. It's easy to prepare, and will warm you up quickly.

1/2 cup chopped onion	Sauté the onions in the safflower oil until translucent. Purée the tofu in a food processor. (If you are puréeing the tofu in a blender, put 1/2 to 3/4 cup of the vegetable stock or water in the blender first and gradually add the tofu.)
2 Tbsp. safflower oil	
8 oz. tofu	
4 cups vegetable stock or water	
1 1/2 cups sauerkraut	
1 clove garlic, minced	Add all ingredients, except the peas, to the onions, and simmer for 30 minutes. Adjust the seasoning, depending on the strength of the sauerkraut. Add the peas, and heat 5 minutes more.
1 tsp. dry mustard	
1 tsp. dill weed	
1/2 tsp. dill seed, crushed	
1/2 tsp. salt	
1/4 tsp. pepper	Serve immediately.
1 cup peas, fresh or frozen	
Yield: 4 servings.	

Curried Carrot Soup

The tastes of orange and raisin in this soup add a slight sweetness that we find especially satisfying on cold autumn and winter days.

2½ large carrots

2 medium onions

3 Tbsp. vegetable oil

2 Tbsp. butter

¼ tsp. garlic powder

½ tsp. curry powder

¾ tsp. salt

¼ cup carrot cooking water

1 tsp. honey

1¼ cups soymilk

2 Tbsp. soy powder (see Glossary) or 1½ Tbsp. flour

½ Tbsp. nutritional yeast

⅓ cup raisins

1 cup water

¼ cup orange juice

¼ tsp. nutmeg, freshly grated

8 oz. tofu

Yield: 4 to 6 servings.

Scrub the carrots. Coarsely chop two of them, and steam until tender (about 10 to 15 minutes).

Dice the onions; grate the remaining ½ carrot. Sauté these over medium heat in the oil and butter until the onions are translucent. Lower the heat, and add the garlic powder, curry powder, and salt to the sautéeing vegetables.

When the steamed carrots are tender, purée them with ¼ cup of the carrot cooking water. With the blender on, *slowly* add the honey and soymilk.

Return to the sautéed onions and carrots, and add the soy powder and yeast, stirring constantly to avoid lumps. Cook this mixture *gently* on low heat for 1 minute. Then add the raisins, and stir in the water.

Pour the carrot-soymilk mixture from the blender slowly into the sauté mixture, stirring as you do so. Add the orange juice and grated fresh nutmeg.

Cut the tofu into ½-inch cubes, and add to soup. Heat gently – do not boil – until the tofu cubes are warmed through.

Miso Squash Soup

A tasty way to make use of squash, this spicy soup is another fall and winter favorite.

1 young butternut squash (approximately 1½ lb.)
3 cups water
2 heaping Tbsp. onion flakes
3 Tbsp. miso
1 cup water
1 Tbsp. Worcestershire sauce
½ tsp. dry mustard
¼ tsp. nutmeg
2 cups water
2 cloves garlic, pressed
1 Tbsp. oil
12 oz. tofu, cut into ½-inch cubes
¼ cup chopped fresh parsley
¼ cup chopped scallions

Yield: 4 to 6 servings.

Scrub the squash, and cut off the stem and blossom-ends. Halve it, and remove the seeds. Cut the squash into large chunks. (If you are cooking a young squash, you will not need to remove the skin; however, if you are cooking an acorn squash or an older butternut squash, the skin will be tough and should be removed.)

Put 3 cups of water in a large saucepan and add the onion flakes. Put in a steamer basket, and add the squash. Steam for 10 to 15 minutes, or until the squash is tender. Reserve 2 cups of the cooking water.

Combine 1 cup of water with the miso in a blender. It will be easier to blend the miso if you add it a little at a time while the blender is on. Once the miso and water are blended smooth, add the Worcestershire sauce, dry mustard and nutmeg. Add some chunks of squash, and blend. Then add the 2 cups of cooking water and more squash, and blend again. Alternate adding 2 more cups water and squash until all the squash is blended. There will probably not be enough room in your blender to add the full amount of water. The remaining water can be added later in the cooking.

In a large saucepan, sauté the pressed garlic in oil until lightly browned.

Add miso-squash mixture and any remaining water and stir. Add the cubed tofu, chopped parsley, and scallions to the soup, and heat until thoroughly warmed, taking care not to boil it.

Tomato Bisque

2 medium onions, thinly sliced

3 cloves garlic, pressed

2 Tbsp. vegetable oil

¾ tsp. salt

2 cups cold water

1 Tbsp. arrowroot, cornstarch or kudzu (optional, but adds to the smooth, creamy texture)

12 oz. tofu

28 oz. can whole tomatoes

1 large ripe fresh tomato, skinned and chopped, or 8-oz. can whole tomatoes

1 stalk celery, finely chopped

fresh parsley, chopped, as garnish

Yield: 4 to 6 servings.

Sauté the thinly sliced onions and pressed garlic in the oil. Add the salt. When translucent and beginning to brown, remove from the heat.

Dissolve the arrowroot in 1 cup of cold water, and then pour into the sautéed onion and garlic mixture. Stir to avoid lumps. Bring to boil over medium heat, stirring occasionally. Reduce heat, and let simmer for 5 minutes.

Break or cut the tofu into small pieces. Purée the 28 oz. of canned tomatoes in the blender, adding the tofu, piece by piece, until smooth. While the blender is still on, slowly add the onion-arrowroot mixture.

When the mixture is very smooth, return it to the saucepan, and add the chopped fresh tomato, and finely chopped celery. Add the remaining cup of water.

Heat gently for 5 to 10 minutes.

Garnish with chopped parsley, and serve immediately.

Asparagus Soup

½ cup mashed tofu
3 cups soymilk
1 lb. asparagus
1 medium onion
2 Tbsp. butter or oil
2 large cloves garlic, pressed
¾ tsp. salt
1 Tbsp. nutritional yeast (optional)
2 Tbsp. soy or wheat flour
¼ cup asparagus-cooking stock
¼ tsp. dried French tarragon
white wine (optional)
hard-cooked egg, finely chopped, as garnish

Yield: 4 servings.

Blend the mashed tofu and soymilk until they are very smooth and creamy. Set aside.

Trim the asparagus, then slice into ¼-inch rounds.

Steam the asparagus until soft (approximately 10 minutes), being careful not to overcook it. Save the stock.

Chop the onion very finely, and sauté it in the butter or oil with the pressed garlic and salt. When they are translucent, add the nutritional yeast and flour. Stir constantly until the flour is lightly browned.

Lower the heat and add the asparagus-cooking stock to the roux, stirring constantly as it thickens. Continue to stir, and *very slowly* add 2 cups of the tofu-soymilk mixture, taking care not to let the liquid come to a boil.

Set aside ¼ cup of cooked asparagus. Add the rest of the asparagus to the 1 cup of tofu-soymilk remaining in the blender. Blend well. Slowly add this to the liquid in the saucepan, stirring constantly.

Add the remaining asparagus and the tarragon.

Increase the heat slightly and cook the soup for 5 to 10 minutes, until all the ingredients are heated through, but *do not let it boil*.

Ladle the soup into individual serving bowls. If desired, add 1 Tbsp. of white wine to each serving, and garnish with chopped hard-cooked egg.

Onion Soup

2 cups chopped onions

¼ cup safflower oil

2 cloves garlic, minced

5 cups water or vegetable stock

½ cup white wine

¼ cup tamari

⅛ tsp. pepper

8 oz. frozen tofu

¼ cup olive oil

2 tsp. garlic salt

grated Parmesan cheese

Yield: 4 to 6 servings.

Preheat oven to 350°

In a soup pot, cook the onions slowly in the safflower oil until soft and translucent. Add the garlic, and cook for 3 minutes. Add the water or stock, white wine, tamari and pepper. Simmer for 40 to 60 minutes.

Defrost the frozen tofu and then squeeze out excess water. Slice the tofu into ¼-inch slices. Mix together the olive oil and garlic salt. Baste the tofu slices with this mixture; then bake on an oiled baking sheet for 20 minutes until crusty.

After the soup has simmered, ladle it into individual oven-proof bowls. Top with a piece of tofu toast sprinkled with Parmesan cheese. Broil until the cheese is golden brown, 3 to 5 minutes. Serve immediately.

Cold Cucumber Tomato Soup

1 medium onion, finely chopped
3 cloves garlic, pressed
1 Tbsp. vegetable oil
1 Tbsp. arrowroot, cornstarch or kudzu
1¼ cups cold water
1 Tbsp. natural soy sauce or tamari
1 large cucumber
2 tomatoes (skinned, if desired)
3 Tbsp. lemon juice
8 oz. tofu, pressed or squeezed
½ tsp. salt
¼ tsp. curry powder
½ tsp. dill weed
¼ cup water
2 Tbsp. finely chopped fresh parsley, or 1 tsp. dried parsley
2 Tbsp. finely chopped fresh basil, or 1 tsp. dried basil

Note: If you wish to skin the tomatoes, immerse them in boiling water for 1 minute and then rinse them in cool water. Then slip off the skins.

Sauté the chopped onion and pressed garlic in the oil until translucent. Set aside.

Dissolve the arrowroot in the cold water and soy sauce. Slowly bring the solution to boil in a small saucepan, stirring occasionally. When the liquid becomes clear and has thickened, remove it from the heat.

Peel the cucumber, and, if desired, cut in half to remove the seeds. Reserve ⅓ of the cucumber for later, and chop the remainder coarsely, along with one of the tomatoes, and put them into a blender. Add to this the lemon juice and the cooled sautéed onions and garlic.

Break or cut the pressed tofu into small pieces, and purée the vegetables in the blender, adding the pieces of tofu, one at a time, until the mixture is smooth. (If the mixture is very thick, add up to ¼ cup of water.)

Add the salt, curry powder, and dill weed. Blend.

While the blender is still on, slowly pour in the cooled arrowroot solution. Add the remaining ¼ cup of water at this point.

When blended and creamy, pour the mixture into a serving bowl.

Dice the remaining tomato and the ⅓ cucumber which you set aside earlier. Chop the parsley and fresh basil very finely. Add these to the mixture in the serving bowl. Chill and serve.

Note: A garnish that will add wonderful color to this soup is marigold petals. Marigolds were developed in the Middle Ages for culinary purposes. If you use them, be sure that they have not been sprayed.

Yield: 4 to 6 servings.

Sweet and Sour Cabbage Soup

This can be prepared quickly, but is even better if it can sit. It's good hot or cold. Try it with a dollop of Tofu Lemon Cream (p. 99), sour cream or yogurt.

1 cup onion, chopped
¼ cup oil
4 cups chopped cabbage
3 cups water
3¼ cups, or 28 oz. can, peeled tomatoes and juice
6 Tbsp. lemon juice
4 Tbsp. honey
½ tsp. salt
⅛ to ¼ tsp. pepper
1 lb. tofu, cut into 1 × ½ -inch pieces

In a soup pot, sauté the onions in the oil for 5 minutes. Add the cabbage, and sauté for 10 minutes more.

Add the water, tomatoes and juice. Simmer for 15 to 20 minutes.

Season the soup with the lemon juice, honey, salt, and pepper. You may wish to increase the amount of salt you add if the canned tomatoes are not pre-salted.

Turn off the heat. Add the cubed tofu, and stir gently. Let the soup sit for 6 to 8 hours before reheating and serving. After this "marrying" period, the tofu will not only have absorbed flavor from the other ingredients in the soup, but it will also be firmer due to the action of the salt and the lemon.

Yield: 5 to 6 servings.

This soup may also be served cold.

Sandwiches

In this section, we have provided recipes which are suitable for serving at different times of the day, and for various occasions from simple to more fancy.

Apple Chutney Sandwiches and Sweet Apple Date Sandwiches (p. 71) are popular for breakfasts and brunches. For those who prefer their first meal to be something heartier and more savory, there is the Grilled Tofu Miso Sandwich (p. 72) to provide a sustained energy boost.

For picnics and large gatherings, we often serve tofalafels, or tofuburgers, which appeal to meat-eaters and vegetarians alike. And when choosing a more sedate form of entertaining, the Open-faced Luncheon Sandwich (p. 73) can provide an elegant, delicately savory and quite satisfying main dish, accompanied by a soup, salad, and light dessert.

Besides the recipes in this section, there are sandwich ideas throughout the cookbook. Be sure to check the Dips, Spreads and Appetizers section for recipes such as Deviled Tofu, Savory Cheese Spread, and Walnut Spinach Paté.

At home we often thaw some frozen tofu and make up the filling of the Egg Rolls II recipe (p. 57). Then we put Tofu Mayonnaise (p. 97) and shredded lettuce into pita bread and have a sandwich that many people have told us tastes like cold turkey, especially on the second day.

And don't forget the possibilities that outdoor barbecuing can offer. Pressed tofu and deep-fried tofu cutlets can be marinated in one of several of the barbecue sauces listed, then cooked outside over a charcoal grill.

Leftovers can make good sandwiches, too. Any of the tofu loaves (see Entrées) can be packed into a lunch box on the following day. Two of my favorite sandwiches consist of:
1) leftover Oven-cooked Barbecue Tofu (p. 115) on a piece of toasted whole wheat bread spread with Dijon or Kosciusko mustard and served with fresh Boston lettuce; 2) Walnut Spinach

Tofu Paté (p. 44) served on a toasted whole wheat English muffin spread with Tofu Mayonnaise and horseradish or mustard and topped with thin slices of Muenster cheese, then broiled until the cheese melts and the sandwich is heated through.

And then there is a deep-fried tofu cutlet, sprinkled with a little natural soy sauce or lemon juice and eaten in a sandwich with mayonnaise, lettuce and tomato, or...

Apple Chutney Sandwich

Try this sandwich when you want something different for breakfast. Mango chutney is usually available at specialty food stores, or in supermarket gourmet sections. It may be a bit too highly seasoned for some children.

4 slices whole wheat toast	Brush the slices of toast with honey and then with chutney.
honey	
mango chutney	Put a slice of tofu on each slice of toast.
8 oz. tofu, cut into ¼- to ½-inch slices	Slather the tofu slices with mango chutney, and layer the apple slices on top of this. Brush the apple slices lightly with honey.
apples, thinly sliced to cover toast (1 or 2 apples)	
Yield: 4 open-faced sandwiches.	Broil the sandwiches until the apples are soft, about 5 to 8 minutes.

Sweet Apple Date Sandwich

For breakfast, brunch or snacktime . . .

8 oz. tofu, cut into ¼- to ½-inch slices	Sauté the tofu slices in butter for about 3 minutes on each side.
butter	Brush the tofu and toast slices with honey, and sprinkle both with cinnamon or nutmeg, or both, whatever you prefer.
4 slices whole wheat or raisin toast	
honey	
cinnamon or nutmeg	
1 cup chopped dates	Place the sautéed tofu slices on the toast, and cover with the chopped dates.
apples, thinly sliced to cover toast (1 or 2 apples)	
	Layer apple slices on the top, and drizzle with honey.
	Broil until the apples are tender, about 5 to 8 minutes.
Yield: 4 open-faced sandwiches.	Serve immediately.

Grilled Tofu Miso Sandwich

The grilled miso imparts a strong and hearty flavor to this sandwich. It's delicious with a crisp green salad and vinaigrette dressing.

8 oz. tofu

2 Tbsp. and 2 tsp. miso

1 Tbsp. and 1 tsp. oil

butter or soy margarine

4 slices of bread

scallions, finely chopped

Yield: 4 open-faced sandwiches.

Slice the cake of tofu into four 1/3 to 1/2-inch slices. Mix together the miso and oil. This mixture will be thick. Spread the tofu slices with the miso-oil mixture. Broil on an oiled sheet without turning about 8 to 10 minutes until hot and fragrant.

Spread four slices of bread with margarine or butter and Tofu Mayonnaise or Garlic Mayonnaise (p. 97). Sprinkle with finely chopped scallions. Top with the broiled tofu slices.

Mushroom Caps on Rye Toast

mushroom caps, enough to cover 4 slices of toast

olive oil, to brush mushroom caps and toast

1 1/3 cups crumbled tofu

3 to 4 tsp. olive oil

1/2 tsp. garlic powder

salt to taste

pepper to taste

4 slices rye toast

3/4 cup grated Cheddar cheese

Yield: 4 open-faced sandwiches.

Brush the mushroom caps with olive oil, and broil for 3 to 4 minutes.

Mix the crumbled tofu with the 3 to 4 tsp. of olive oil, garlic powder, salt and pepper.

Brush the slices of rye toast with olive oil.

Spread crumbled tofu mixture on the toast slices.

Put the mushroom caps, hollow-side down, on top of the tofu mixture, and cover them with the grated Cheddar cheese.

Broil the sandwiches until the cheese is melted and the tofu is hot, about 5 minutes.

Open-Faced Luncheon Sandwich

This is one of our favorite sandwich recipes, very suitable for a luncheon entrée.

4 English muffins, halved	Preheat oven to 350°.
3 Tbsp. butter or margarine	Lightly toast the English muffins, spread with butter and set aside.
1¼ cups mashed tofu	
1 medium stalk celery, diced	Combine mashed tofu, celery, parsley, pressed garlic, oil, thyme, soy sauce and Worcestershire sauce, mixing well with a fork to blend flavors thoroughly.
3 Tbsp. finely chopped fresh parsley	
1 clove garlic, pressed	
2 Tbsp. olive oil or cold-pressed corn oil	Mound 2 to 3 Tbsp. of the tofu mixture on the top of each buttered half of a muffin. Place in a shallow baking dish, topping each sandwich with a generous amount of grated cheese. Bake for 15 to 20 minutes at 350°, or until the sandwiches are warmed through and the cheese is melted and delicately browned. Garnish with parsley and serve immediately.
scant ½ tsp. dried thyme	
2 Tbsp. natural soy sauce or tamari	
2 tsp. Worcestershire sauce	
½ to ⅔ cup grated mild cheese	
parsley, as garnish	
Yield: 8 open-faced sandwiches, or 4 servings.	

Broiled Tomato Curry Sandwich

8 oz. tofu	Slice the tofu into 4 slices, ¼ to ½-inch thick. In a large skillet, heat the oil, soy sauce and garlic. Add the tofu slices and sauté until lightly browned on both sides.
2 to 3 Tbsp. olive oil	
2 to 3 Tbsp. natural soy sauce or tamari	
1 to 2 cloves garlic, minced	
4 slices rye bread	Toast the rye bread slices, then lightly spread with Dijon mustard. Put on the sautéed tofu, and sprinkle with curry powder.
Dijon mustard	
curry powder	
2 tomatoes	Slice the tomatoes, and divide the slices among the four pieces of toast. Top each sandwich with ¼ cup of grated cheese.
1 cup grated cheese	
	Broil until the cheese is melted. Serve hot.
Yield: 4 open-faced sandwiches.	

Broiled Zucchini Rosemary Sandwich

1 medium zucchini
8 oz. tofu
2 to 3 Tbsp. olive oil
1 Tbsp. lemon juice
2 cloves garlic, minced
2/3 tsp. ground rosemary
4 slices whole wheat bread, toasted
salt to taste
1/2 cup grated Parmesan cheese

Slice the zucchini thinly into 1/8- to 1/4-inch slices. You will need enough slices to cover four slices of toast. Slice the tofu into four 1/4- to 1/2-inch slices.

In a large skillet, heat the oil, lemon juice, garlic, and rosemary. Then add the sliced zucchini and sauté lightly. Remove the zucchini with a slotted spoon, and set aside. In the same oil mixture, sauté the tofu slices until golden brown on both sides.

Toast the bread, and brush lightly with olive oil. Put on the sautéed tofu slices, followed by the zucchini slices. Lightly salt the zucchini, then cover each sandwich with 2 Tbsp. (or more) grated Parmesan cheese.

Broil until the Parmesan is golden brown.

Yield: 4 open-faced sandwiches.

Tofuburgers I

This tofuburger recipe calls for frozen tofu (p. 19). Once you've thawed it, which takes about 15 minutes, you can prepare this recipe in no time.

1 cup of mixed diced mushrooms, onions and celery
8 to 10 oz. frozen tofu, thawed and squeezed
1 Tbsp. butter or oil
2 eggs
1/4 cup tomato or V-8 juice
1 to 1 1/2 Tbsp. vegetable or beef bouillon powder
3/4 to 1 cup bread crumbs to bind the mixture

Sauté the diced vegetables in the butter or oil until tender. Set aside to cool.

Place the thawed tofu in a bowl and mash it up with a fork. Add the eggs, the tomato or V-8 juice, and the cooled diced vegetables. Mix well.

Add the bouillon powder, to taste, and enough bread crumbs to bind the mixture.

Form into 5 or 6 burger-shaped patties. (The patties may be formed, covered, and chilled to fry later, if necessary.)

Fry in a skillet with oil or butter until well-browned on both sides (about 5 to 10 minutes per side). Serve on buns with your favorite condiments.

Yield: 5 to 6 patties; 3 servings.

Tofuburgers II

As all burgers seem to be, these, too, are very popular with children.

2 lb. tofu

1 medium onion, finely chopped

2 Tbsp. safflower oil

3 eggs

1 cup bread crumbs

½ to 1 tsp. garlic powder

½ to 1 tsp. onion powder

¼ cup natural soy sauce

safflower oil to oil baking sheet and brush patties

Drain the tofu for about 15 to 20 minutes, then press it while the onions are cooking.

Preheat the oven to 350°.

Sauté the chopped onion in the safflower oil until translucent.

Mash the pressed tofu. Add the sautéed onions and the remaining ingredients, except oil for baking sheet, to the mashed tofu. Mix well.

Oil a baking sheet with safflower oil. Form the tofu mixture into 4 to 6 patties. Brush safflower oil on the tops of the burgers.

Bake for 50 minutes. When the burgers are firm and brown on one side after about 25 minutes, turn to brown the other side for the remaining 25 minutes.

Yield: 4 to 6 servings.   Serve on buns with the works!

Tofalafels

These are good hot or cold, and great for serving to people who have never eaten tofu.

TOFALAFELS:

2 lb. tofu, pressed or squeezed

½ cup minced onion

½ cup sesame seeds

½ cup bread crumbs

2 Tbsp. tahini

2 tsp. cumin

2 tsp. natural soy sauce or tamari

1¾ tsp. garlic powder

1 tsp. salt

¼ tsp. cayenne

sesame oil

ACCOMPANIMENTS:

pita bread

chopped tomatoes

green salad fixings

yogurt dressing

Yield: 4 to 6 servings.

Preheat the oven to 325°.

Mash the tofu. Add the remaining tofalafel ingredients, and mix thoroughly.

Form into 1-inch balls, and place on oiled baking sheets.

Brush the totalafels with sesame oil.

Bake for 35 to 40 minutes. When the tofalafels have browned on one side after about 20 minutes, turn to brown the other side for the remainder of the cooking time.

Serve hot in warm pita bread with tomatoes, green salad, and a yogurt dressing of equal parts yogurt and tahini (½ cup is a good amount), with lemon juice to taste.

Grilled Eggplant Tofu Sandwich

1 medium eggplant

salt

olive oil

8 oz. tofu

4 slices bread

Garlic Mayonnaise (p. 97)

4 Tbsp. Parmesan cheese

Cut the eggplant into slices ½-inch thick, and remove the peel. The slices should be as large as the bread you are planning to use.

Salt each slice of the eggplant with ½ to 1 tsp. of salt. Set aside for a couple of hours so that the salt can draw out the bitterness from the eggplant. The eggplant will shrink during this process.

Afterwards, rinse the eggplant, and gently squeeze dry. The slices will be limp.

Brush the eggplant slices with olive oil on both sides, and put on an oiled baking sheet.

Slice the cake of tofu into quarters lengthwise. Each slice will be approximately ½-inch thick. Brush each slice on both sides with olive oil, sprinkle with salt, and put on the baking sheet with the eggplant.

Broil the eggplant and tofu 8 to 10 minutes per side, or until they begin to be brown and fragrant. Be careful not to break the tofu slices when turning them.

Thickly spread the bread slices with Garlic Mayonnaise. Put on the eggplant, then the tofu. Sprinkle the top of each sandwich with 1 Tbsp. of Parmesan cheese.

Transfer the sandwiches onto a baking sheet or piece of foil, and broil again for a few minutes or until the Parmesan turns golden.

Yield: 4 open-faced sandwiches.

Serve hot.

Hero Sandwich

This sandwich can be made with regular tofu or Deep-fried Tofu Cutlets (p. 166), depending on the texture you prefer. The marinade keeps well, and can be used a number of times. Have some on hand, so you can start marinating your tofu in the morning. By lunch time you will have little to do but put the sandwich together and enjoy it.

4 slices pressed or unpressed tofu, ¼- to ½-inch thick, or 4 slices deep-fried tofu cutlets of same size

8 slices of bread, or 2 submarine buns

Tofu Mayonnaise, Garlic Mayonnaise (p. 97), or butter

onion slices

tomato slices

pickles

lettuce

MARINADE:

¼ cup catsup

¼ cup vinegar

¼ cup natural soy sauce

¼ cup water

1 Tbsp. and 1 tsp. Dijon mustard

Yield: 4 sandwiches or 2 submarine sandwiches.

Press tofu, if you wish. Combine the marinade ingredients. Marinate the tofu or tofu cutlets for at least two hours. If you are using deep-fried tofu cutlets, lightly score the top and bottom or cut a small slit in each end of the cutlet so that the marinade can penetrate more easily.

After the tofu has marinated, spread the slices of bread with your favorite mayonnaise, or use butter.

Pile on slices of onions, tomatoes, pickles, marinated tofu, and lettuce. (If you are using submarine buns, you may wish to use two slices of marinated tofu per bun.)

To make hot sandwiches, toast the bread slices or submarine buns, and broil the marinated tofu for 8 to 10 minutes on an oiled cookie sheet, basting with the marinade if you prefer. Then assemble sandwiches as above.

Salads

As in the other recipe sections, the recipes here are loosely arranged according to the length of preparation time. Those which require marinating will be grouped together as a reminder that additional time, albeit little additional effort, is necessary. Remember to save your marinades. They can be re-used.

Many salads make great entrées. We have the good fortune to be invited to quite a few potluck picnics and dinners, and have found that regardless of the group of people involved, salads such as the Avocado Tofu, the Tofu Cauliflower and the Crown Jewel Salad are much enjoyed.

Again, you may wish to introduce tofu into salads of your own creation. Finely cubed or diced tofu is a simple and appropriate choice for many salads. Deep-fried Tofu Cubes (p. 167), whole or thinly sliced, may be used in this way or in marinated salads where they soak up seasonings and also contribute a most pleasant texture.

Avocado Tofu Salad

Delicious taste and ease of preparation both contribute to placing this salad high on our list of favorites.

8 oz. tofu	
1 medium avocado	
1 medium or 2 small tomatoes	
1 large cucumber	

DRESSING:

¼ cup olive oil
3 Tbsp. soy sauce
8 oz. tofu
¼ cup lemon juice
1 small onion, diced

Yield: 4 to 6 servings.

Cut the vegetables and tofu into ½-inch cubes. Lightly salt the tomatoes.

Combine all the dressing ingredients in a blender.

Mix the vegetables and dressing together gently, and serve on a bed of lettuce or alfalfa sprouts.

Garbanzo Tofu Walnut Salad

1 lb. cooked garbanzo beans, coarsely mashed
8 oz. tofu, cut into ½-inch cubes
⅔ cup finely chopped walnuts

DRESSING:

½ cup lemon juice
6 Tbsp. olive oil
3 cloves garlic, crushed
1½ tsp. salt

Yield: 4 to 6 servings.

Combine the salad ingredients; mix together the dressing ingredients.

Pour the dressing over the salad ingredients, and toss lightly, but *thoroughly*.

Mound the salad on a bed of lettuce, and serve.

Tofu Tomato Fans

This salad is one of our favorites during the height of the tomato season. It can be used as either a main dish or a salad.

DRESSING:

¼ cup finely chopped fresh parsley

¼ cup mashed tofu

2 Tbsp. lemon juice

1 tsp. basil

¼ tsp. salt

SALAD:

2 very large tomatoes

8 oz. tofu

1 Tbsp. Dijon mustard

1 Tbsp. natural soy sauce or tamari

3 Tbsp. safflower oil

2 hard-cooked eggs

Yield: 2 servings.

When I make this recipe, I prepare the dressing first so that the flavors have more time to blend. Combine all the dressing ingredients in a food processor or blender, and blend until smooth. Set aside.

Core the tomatoes, then, leaving the bottom ¼-inch of each tomato intact, cut down from the top in ¼-inch slices. Lightly salt the cut sections.

Cut the tofu into slices roughly 1½ × 1½ × ½ inch. Mix together the mustard and natural soy sauce. Brush the tofu slices with this mixture. Lightly pan-fry the tofu slices in the safflower oil until there is a golden crust on both sides.

Peel the eggs, then slice them into thin slices.

To assemble the fans, alternate tofu and egg slices in between the tomato slices. Spoon the dressing in between the slices and lightly over the tops of the tomatoes. If you wish, garnish with parsley sprigs or chopped fresh chives.

Mushroom Tofu Salad

For a change, instead of dressing the salad with soy sauce, try it with your favorite mixture of oil, vinegar, and herbs.

4 cups thinly sliced mushrooms
1 Tbsp. olive oil
4 Tbsp. natural soy sauce or tamari
2 cups green beans, cut into 1½-inch pieces
8 oz. tofu, cut into ½-inch cubes
3 cups water
2 scallions, finely chopped
soy sauce to taste
⅓ cup finely chopped watercress

Yield: 4 servings.

Lightly sauté mushrooms in the olive oil. After they are cooked, add 1 Tbsp. of soy sauce to them.

Steam the green bean slices until they are crisp-tender, about 6 minutes.

Parboil the tofu in the water with 3 Tbsp. of soy sauce for 5 minutes. Lift out tofu cubes with a slotted spoon or wire mesh strainer, and put into a serving dish.

Add the mushrooms, green beans, and scallions. Mix gently, seasoning to taste with soy sauce.

Sprinkle the chopped watercress over the top of the salad, and serve.

Basic Tofu Cheese

This recipe tastes best if eaten the day it is prepared. For people who cannot eat dairy products, this dish can be used as one would use cottage cheese.

1 lb. tofu, drained
2 Tbsp. oil (olive or sesame, preferred)
1 Tbsp. and 1 tsp. lemon juice or vinegar
¾ tsp. Worcestershire sauce
¼ rounded tsp. salt
pinch garlic powder (optional)

Yield: 3 to 4 servings.

Mash the tofu; then add the remaining ingredients, and mix well.

Chill for an hour or so to allow the flavors to blend.

Mung Bean Sprout Salad with Ginger Dressing

1 lb. tofu
1/2 cup slivered almonds
1 small head Boston lettuce
2 cups mung bean sprouts
2 cups alfalfa sprouts
1 cup finely chopped scallions
1 cup chopped watercress

MARINADE FOR TOFU CUBES:

1 tsp. freshly grated ginger root
2 Tbsp. natural soy sauce or tamari

GINGER DRESSING:

1/4 cup lemon juice
2 Tbsp. natural soy sauce or tamari
2 Tbsp. sesame oil
1 Tbsp. rice vinegar
2 rounded Tbsp. freshly grated ginger root
8 oz. tofu
1/2 cup chopped scallions

Yield: 8 to 10 servings;
1 1/2 cups dressing.

Lightly press the tofu for 10 minutes (p.22). Then cut the pressed tofu into 1/2-inch cubes.

Prepare the marinade by combining the grated ginger and the soy sauce in a bowl large enough to hold the tofu cubes.

Add the tofu cubes to the marinade, and gently toss them, taking care not to break them up.

Toast the slivered almonds either in the oven or on top of the stove until they are a warm golden color. Set them aside.

Tear the lettuce leaves into bite-sized pieces, and put into a large salad bowl. Add the mung bean and alfalfa sprouts, the scallions, and watercress.

To prepare the ginger dressing, combine in a blender the lemon juice, soy sauce, sesame oil, rice vinegar, and the grated ginger root. Add the tofu gradually to the other ingredients and make sure the ginger is completely blended in with the other ingredients and the consistency is very smooth.

After the ginger has been completely blended in, add the chopped scallions, and blend lightly for a few seconds.

Remove the tofu cubes from the marinade. Add the tofu, cooled almonds, and dressing to the rest of the salad, and toss lightly.

Serve immediately.

Corn Tofu Salad with French Dressing

This salad does not last long in our house, especially when we have fresh corn available. It's a wonderful way to use up fresh corn before it goes stale. This recipe can be prepared fairly quickly even though deep-frying is called for.

SALAD:

8 oz. tofu

2 cups fresh or defrosted frozen corn

2 Tbsp. oil

2 tsp. lemon juice

salt

3 Tbsp. finely chopped pimento

2 Tbsp. minced sweet Bermuda onion

FRENCH DRESSING:

¼ cup olive oil

3 Tbsp. lemon juice

½ tsp. Dijon mustard

1 Tbsp. minced parsley

1 clove garlic, minced

GARNISH:

3 long slices pimento

paprika

Yield: 4 servings.

Press the tofu for at least 30 minutes. Then cut it into pieces approximately ¾ × ¾ × ½ inches. Prepare as you would deep-fried tofu cubes (p. 167).

While the tofu cubes are still hot, toss them gently with lemon juice and salt.

Put the corn into a serving bowl, and add the tofu cubes and remaining salad ingredients to it.

Mix together all the dressing ingredients.

Add the dressing to the salad ingredients, and toss lightly.

Smooth the top of the salad, and arrange the pimento slices in the center of the salad. As a variation you may also wish to serve the salad in a shallow bowl on a bed of lettuce leaves.

Sprinkle lightly with paprika and serve.

Confetti Salad

1½ cups shredded red cabbage

1 cup crisp fresh lettuce, thinly cut

1 cup fresh spinach, coarsely chopped

1 small red onion, thinly sliced

1 cup Basic Tofu Cheese (p. 82)

¼ cup chopped black olives

¼ cup walnut pieces

Yield: 4 servings.

Place all the ingredients in a mixing bowl. Toss lightly. Serve in individual bowls with Tarragon Dressing (p. 97).

Stuffed Cucumber Boats

3 small cucumbers (4 to 6 inches long)

2 cups mashed tofu

3 Tbsp. olive oil

2 Tbsp. and 1 tsp. lemon juice

2½ Tbsp. finely chopped shallots

1 tsp. natural soy sauce or tamari

½ tsp. dried dill weed (or 1 Tbsp. finely chopped fresh dill)

scant ¼ tsp. salt

lettuce, as serving bed for cucumbers

parsley, finely chopped, as garnish

Yield: 4 to 6 servings.

Pare the cucumbers to remove skins. Slice in half lengthwise, and scoop out the seeds.

To the mashed tofu add the olive oil, lemon juice, shallots, soy sauce, dill weed, salt, and mix thoroughly.

Mound the filling into the hollowed-out cucumbers.

Chill before serving to allow the flavors to blend together.

Serve on a bed of lettuce garnished with finely chopped parsley.

Note: To serve this recipe as a canapé, do not hollow out the cucumbers. Simply slice them thinly, put a dollop of the tofu stuffing on top, and garnish with a sliced olive round. They can be served with thin wheat crackers.

Stuffed Tomatoes

6 medium tomatoes
salt
2½ cups mashed tofu
3 Tbsp. sesame oil
1½ Tbsp. lemon juice
1 Tbsp. rice wine vinegar*
2 tsp. natural soy sauce or tamari
¼ tsp. garlic powder
¼ tsp. salt
dash Tabasco sauce
⅔ cup fresh chives, chopped
2 heaping Tbsp. fresh parsley, very finely chopped
parsley, as garnish (optional)
lettuce, as serving bed for tomatoes
*If rice wine vinegar is unavailable, add an additional ½ Tbsp. of lemon juice. (Lemon juice is more overpowering, so only half as much is used.)
Yield: 6 stuffed tomatoes.

Skin the tomatoes (p. 67). Then cut out the stem section, and slice off the tops. Save these.

Hollow out the tomatoes, saving the insides for tomato sauces, soups, etc. Lightly sprinkle the insides of the hollowed-out tomatoes with salt, and invert them.

Prepare the stuffing by adding to the mashed tofu all the remaining ingredients, except the chives, parsley, and lettuce. Mix thoroughly.

Add the chives and parsley to the tofu mixture, and mix well.

Fill the tomato hollows with the stuffing. Cover with the tomato slices you set aside earlier. The stuffed tomatoes can be garnished with parsley and served on a bed of lettuce, but first they should be chilled for an hour or two to allow the flavors to blend.

Tomato Basil Salad

Summer is the time to enjoy this salad . The combination of fresh basil and tomatoes is hard to beat.

8 oz. tofu
5 cups chopped tomatoes
½ tsp. salt
½ cup chopped fresh basil
1 small red onion sliced
2 Tbsp. lemon juice
⅓ cup olive oil
⅛ tsp. pepper (optional)
Yield: 4 to 6 servings.

Press the tofu for 20 to 30 minutes. Salt the tomatoes, and let them sit in a serving bowl for 20 minutes.

Cut the tofu into ¼-inch cubes.

Add the tofu, basil, onions and lemon juice to the tomatoes. Toss lightly. Chill for one to two hours. Just before serving, add the olive oil, and, if desired, the pepper.

Cucumber Age Salad

Another recipe from Soja in Toronto. It is hard to stop eating this one.

3 regular cucumbers, or
1½ English cucumbers

½ to 1 tsp. salt

5 deep-fried tofu pouches
(see Glossary and pp. 166 to 167
for instructions on making
pouches at home)

BROTH:

2 quarts water

2 pieces kombu (see Glossary)

½ cup natural soy sauce
or tamari

¼ cup sake

1½ Tbsp. honey

DRESSING:

10 oz. tofu, pressed or
squeezed (p. 22)

1½ tsp. honey, or more to taste

1¼ Tbsp. natural soy sauce
or tamari

¼ cup rice wine vinegar

1½ oz. sesame seeds, roasted

Yield: 4 to 6 servings.

Cut the cucumbers in half. If you are using regular cucumbers, remove their seeds. Slice the cucumber halves as thinly as possible, then lightly salt them. Let them sit for 20 minutes, then wring them out by wrapping the cucumbers in a fresh towel, and squeezing them out.

Prepare the broth for simmering the tofu pouches by bringing the water and kombu pieces to boil for 1 minute. Then remove the kombu. Add the tamari, sake and honey. (This broth will keep indefinitely in the refrigerator.)

Cut five deep-fried tofu pouches into ½-inch squares. Place them in a frying pan, pour enough broth over them to cover, and simmer for about 10 to 15 minutes, or until all the broth has been absorbed.

Put all dressing ingredients into a blender or food processor, and blend until smooth. If you are using a blender, break the tofu into small pieces, then add to the other dressing ingredients.

Combine the sliced cucumbers, tofu-pouch pieces, and 1 cup of the dressing. The remaining dressing can be used to freshen up the salad if you have any left on the next day (the salad will keep 2 to 3 days) or it may be used as a dressing for tossed vegetable salads.

Tomato Aspic Salad

4 oz. tofu, pressed
2 tsp. natural soy sauce or tamari
2 tsp. lemon juice
16-oz. can V-8 or tomato juice
1 vegetable bouillon cube
1/2 tsp. Worcestershire sauce
1 1/4 tsp. agar-agar powder
1/2 tsp. dried basil
1/2 tsp. dried dill weed
4 ice cubes
1 Tbsp. finely chopped mild onion
1 small stalk celery, thinly sliced
1 Tbsp. finely chopped chives

Cut the pressed tofu into 1/2-inch cubes, and place in a small bowl.

Pour soy sauce and lemon juice over the tofu, toss lightly, and set aside.

Combine in a 1-quart saucepan 1 cup of V-8 juice, the bouillon cube, Worcestershire sauce, and agar-agar powder. Bring to boil over medium heat, stirring occasionally to prevent the agar-agar from sticking to the bottom of the pan.

When the mixture boils, reduce heat, and add the basil, dill weed, and the remaining cup of V-8 juice. Simmer for 5 minutes, stirring once or twice.

When the 5 minutes are up, remove the agar-agar mixture from the heat, and set saucepan in a large, shallow pan of cold water.

Add 4 ice cubes to the hot aspic, and stir to dissolve. When the aspic begins to set (5 to 10 minutes), add the onion, celery, and drained tofu cubes, stirring carefully to avoid breaking the tofu.

Pour the aspic into four 8 oz. serving dishes, garnishing tops with chives.

This aspic gels at room temperature in less than 1/2 hour and can be served then or chilled for use later in the day.

Because of the presence of the vegetable and tofu pieces, it does not unmold well. We suggest that you serve it directly from the dishes into which it was poured.

Yield: 4 servings.

Summer Macaroni Salad

4 large tomatoes
1 sweet red pepper
8 oz. tofu
20 leaves fresh basil
2 to 4 cloves garlic, pressed
1/2 cup olive oil
1 tsp. salt
pepper to taste
1 lb. corkscrew macaroni
grated Parmesan cheese, to taste

Yield: 4 to 6 servings.

Cut the tomatoes into 1 1/2-inch chunks, the red pepper into thin strips, and the tofu into 1-inch cubes. Tear the basil leaves in half.

Combine all ingredients, except the macaroni and Parmesan, and marinate for at least two hours. Stir occasionally.

Cook the macaroni al dente, or until it offers slight resistance to biting down on it, but no longer has the taste of raw flour. Drain well.

Add the macaroni to the marinated vegetables and tofu. Mix well, sprinkle with Parmesan, and serve immediately.

Sweet and Sour Cucumber Noodle Salad

SALAD:

2 oz. cellophane noodles
1 small cucumber
8 oz. tofu
1/2 cup chopped tomato
Romaine lettuce, as bed for salad

DRESSING:

1/4 cup honey
1/3 cup cider vinegar
1/8 tsp. salt
1/8 tsp. garlic powder

Yield: 4 servings.

Cook noodles. Dampen work surface and spread out noodles into a square shape (about 10 inches). Cut through noodles at 2-inch intervals in each of 3 directions (p. 92).

Cut cucumber into 1/4-inch rounds, and the tofu into 1/2-inch cubes.

Mix all dressing ingredients together, and heat in a saucepan until just simmering.

Add hot dressing to cucumbers, tofu, and noodles.

Refrigerate for several hours.

Just before you are ready to serve the salad add the chopped tomato to it.

Serve on a bed of lettuce.

Marinated Tofu Rice Salad

MARINADE:

¼ cup olive oil

3 Tbsp. lemon juice

SALAD:

1½ cups cooked rice, cooked with 2 Tbsp. of lemon juice

2 cups sliced mushrooms

½ large red pepper, thinly sliced

½ cup black Greek olives (oil-cured olives)

8 oz. tofu

3 Tbsp. natural soy sauce or tamari

½ cup walnuts

Yield: 4 to 6 servings.

Prepare the marinade.

While the rice is still hot, add the sliced mushrooms, pepper, olives, and marinade. Toss gently to distribute ingredients evenly.

Bring 3 cups of water to boil. Meanwhile cut the tofu into ½-inch cubes. Add the soy sauce to the water, then parboil the tofu cubes in the soy sauce mixture for 5 minutes.

Add the parboiled tofu cubes and the walnuts to the rice mixture. Mix gently so as not to break up the tofu.

Refrigerate for at least two hours to allow the flavors to meld.

Red Tofu Salad with Mustard Dressing

1½ cups peeled, cubed raw beets

1½ cups cubed raw potato

8 oz. tofu, cubed

¼ cup chopped scallions

romaine lettuce as serving bed for salad

MARINADE:

¼ cup cider vinegar

3 Tbsp. olive oil

½ tsp. summer savory

MUSTARD DRESSING:

4 oz. tofu

¼ cup olive oil

2 Tbsp. lemon juice

1 Tbsp. tahini

1 Tbsp. Dijon mustard

¼ tsp. curry

½ tsp. salt (optional)

Yield: 4 servings.

Steam cubed beets until tender (about 15 minutes); steam potatoes until tender, but not mushy (about 10 minutes); steam tofu cubes for 5 minutes.

Prepare marinade, and add it to the hot beets, potatoes, and tofu, mixing thoroughly but gently. Allow marinating vegetables to sit for at least 2 hours.

Prepare mustard dressing by blending all dressing ingredients together in a food processor or blender.

When ready to serve, add the chopped scallions to the marinating vegetables. Mound onto a bed of romaine lettuce. Pour mustard dressing over the peak of the mound.

Crown Jewel Salad

This marinated salad is one of the customer favorites at Rochester's Regular Restaurant. By coarsely cutting the vegetables into bite-size pieces, steaming some until barely tender, and marinating them, the colors of the vegetables are brought to the peak of their individual richness, hence the name ...

The following ingredients are suggestions. The restaurant varies the kind of vegetables used, to some extent, according to season.

8 oz. tofu (or deep-fried tofu cubes)

1 cup broccoli flowerets

1 cup cauliflower flowerets

1 large carrot, cut into ½-inch chunks

1½ cups sliced mushrooms

1 small red onion, thinly sliced

1 cup halved cherry tomatoes

1 cup cooked garbanzo beans

MARINADE:

1 cup olive oil

⅔ cup red wine vinegar

2 Tbsp. lemon juice

2 cloves garlic, pressed

1½ tsp. salt

pinch of each: basil, thyme, oregano, marjoram

Yield: 6 to 8 servings.

Press tofu for 30 minutes, then cut into ½-inch cubes. If you are using deep-fried tofu cubes, see Deep-fried Tofu Cutlets (p. 167). Cut the tofu into ¾-inch cubes before deep frying.

Steam the broccoli flowerets until just tender, 2 to 3 minutes, then plunge them into cold water to stop further cooking; drain. Follow the same procedure with the cauliflower for 3 to 4 minutes and chopped carrots for 5 minutes. The objective here is to intensify the color of the vegetables by light steaming, then to stop cooking suddenly before the vegetables begin to lose their color. Let your eyes help you determine when the vegetables are at their peak.

The mushrooms and red onion may be either lightly steamed or used uncooked.

Combine all ingredients in a large serving bowl. Prepare the marinade, and pour it over the vegetables and tofu. Chill, and marinate for at least two hours. (If you find the marinade a bit too strong, you can dilute it with ¼ cup water.)

Deep-fried Tofu, Noodle and Vegetable Salad

Another inspired creation by one of the cooks at Rochester's Regular Restaurant. Mirin sake, dark sesame oil, saifun or cellophane noodles (see Glossary) can be purchased in oriental food markets or in the oriental sections of large supermarkets.

3¾-oz. package cellophane noodles ("saifun" or "fansee")
water to soak noodles
oil for deep-frying
1½ lb. tofu, pressed
2 quarts boiling water
¾ cup thinly sliced onion
½ cup shredded red cabbage
¾ cup julienned carrots
¾ cup slivered green or red pepper
¾ cup julienned eggplant
½ cup sliced fresh mushrooms
2 to 4 Tbsp. oil
2 Tbsp. dark sesame oil
2 Tbsp. vinegar
2 Tbsp. honey
2 Tbsp. natural soy sauce
2 Tbsp. mirin sake
2 Tbsp. sesame seeds, roasted

Soak the cellophane noodles in water for 30 minutes.

Fill a deep-sided pan, wok or deep-fryer with oil to a level of 1½ to 2 inches. Heat the oil to a temperature between 350° and 375° (see pp. 23 to 26).

Cut the pressed tofu into 1 × ½ × ½-inch pieces. Deep-fry until lightly browned, about 1½ minutes, taking care not to cook too many pieces at once. Remove and drain on a rack covered with paper towel.

Remove the noodles from the soaking water, drain and drop into 2 quarts of rapidly boiling water. Cook the noodles for 10 minutes after the water comes to a boil. Drain and rinse the noodles with cool water. Then allow them to drain again for 15 minutes.

While the noodles are cooking, sauté the vegetables separately, one kind at a time until they are just tender. Set aside to cool.

Dampen work surface and spread out noodles into a square shape (about 10 inches). Cut through noodles at 2-inch intervals in each of 3 directions (see diagram).

Place cut noodles in a bowl with sautéed vegetables and tofu. Toss gently. Season with dark sesame oil, vinegar, honey, soy sauce and mirin. Toss lightly, taste, and add additional amounts of the seasonings as desired to suit taste.

Turn salad into an attractive serving bowl, and garnish with roasted sesame seeds. Serve either at room temperature or chilled.

Yield: 6 to 8 servings.

Tofu Cauliflower Salad

1½ cups cauliflower flowerets

2 cups green beans

8 oz. tofu

1 avocado

⅓ cup finely chopped parsley

MARINADE/DRESSING:

½ cup olive oil

¼ cup cider vinegar

½ tsp. salt

¼ tsp. thyme

1 medium clove garlic, crushed

pinch cayenne

Break the cauliflower into small flowerets. Slice the green beans diagonally into 1½-inch lengths, and cut tofu into ½-inch cubes.

Steam the cauliflower and then the green beans until tender, but still crisp. Set aside, keeping the green beans and cauliflower separate.

Steam the tofu for 5 minutes. (If tofu is steamed for too long, it will become rubbery.)

Combine the steamed cauliflower and tofu in a bowl.

Prepare the marinade, and divide it evenly between the green beans and the cauliflower-tofu. Gently mix the marinade with the ingredients in the two bowls.

Marinate the beans and cauliflower-tofu for several hours, stirring occasionally during that time.

After several hours have passed, combine the marinated green beans and cauliflower-tofu.

Cube the avocado and with the parsley add to the marinated ingredients.

Yield: 4 to 6 servings.

The salad may be served immediately.

Dressings and Sauces

Tofu's delicate, lightly sweet flavor and highly absorbent quality make it suitable as an accompaniment for all kinds of sauces and dressings. When added to sauces or broths, it takes on the flavor of these various liquids and adds body and protein as well without injecting an overriding flavor of its own.

This section begins with a list of salad dressings, dipping, cooked and sweet sauces which appear with other recipes in the book, and which could be used as dressings for salads, main dishes or desserts of your own creation. Following this list are recipes for additional salad dressings. One point to remember about these dressings is that although they can be served immediately, they are better if they can be chilled for an hour or so before using.

Dipping sauces come next. They can be used with freshly made, steamed or parboiled tofu, deep- or pan-fried tofu and with tempura. Two of the simplest and tastiest of all dipping sauces are natural soy sauce or tamari. Try these with freshly made tofu, adding, to taste, lemon juice, dark sesame oil and condiments such as finely sliced scallions and onions, slivered or minced fresh ginger root, finely sliced red radishes or daikon (large white Japanese radish), thinly sliced nori or pickled vegetables. Using any of these dipping sauces along with your favorite kind of tofu and condiments will give you a simple and nutritious meal in no time.

Cooked sauces and sweet sauces and dressings follow the dipping sauces.

Tofu can be blended into almost any dressing or sauce to give it added substance and protein without affecting the flavor. In dishes where you substitute tofu or soymilk for dairy products, you will be contributing no cholesterol and a much lower fat and sodium content without losing a significant amount of protein.

Tofu may also be crumbled or finely diced and added to dressings for a cheese-like texture. Try it the next time you make Roquefort dressing.

Dressings and Sauces
Included in Other Recipes
in Cook with Tofu

Tofu Mayonnaise

Try this tofu mayonnaise, a recipe of Toronto's Soja Soyfood Café.

1 cup mashed tofu
2½ Tbsp. light vegetable oil
2½ Tbsp. cider vinegar
1 tsp. Dijon mustard
½ tsp. salt
dash pepper
Yield: approximately 1½ cups.

Blend all ingredients in a food processor or blender until very smooth. Keep refrigerated (this mayonnaise will keep in the refrigerator for 10 to 14 days).

Garlic Mayonnaise

This light mayonnaise works well as a spread on sandwiches, or as a simple salad dressing.

1 cup soymilk
½ cup olive oil
1 clove garlic, pressed
2 tsp. vinegar
1 tsp. honey
¼ tsp. dried mustard
¼ tsp. salt
Yield: 1½ cups.

Pour the soymilk into a blender. Turn the blender on to low speed, and slowly drizzle in the olive oil.

With the blender still on, add the remaining ingredients.

Chill before serving.

Tarragon Dressing

¼ cup oil (olive or light vegetable)
¼ cup water
2 Tbsp. wine vinegar
1 heaping tsp. dried tarragon
8 oz. tofu
Yield: 1½ cups.

Combine all ingredients in a blender, except the tofu.

Cut or break the tofu into small pieces. With the blender on, add it, piece by piece, until it is all blended, and the dressing is very smooth.

Russian Dressing

3½ Tbsp. catsup
¼ cup water
2 Tbsp. lemon juice
2 Tbsp. olive oil
1 tsp. wine vinegar
1 tsp. Worcestershire sauce
1 heaping Tbsp. finely grated onion
2 tsp. horseradish
¼ tsp. salt
8 oz. tofu
Yield: 1¾ cups.

Combine all ingredients in a blender, except the tofu.

Cut or break the tofu into small pieces. With the blender on, add it, piece by piece, until all is blended, and the dressing has a very smooth consistency.

Creamy Tofu Herb Dressing

This creamy dressing is a popular choice of customers at the Regular Restaurant in Rochester, which is known for its high-quality salads.

3 Tbsp. lemon juice
1 Tbsp. natural soy sauce or tamari
1 Tbsp. safflower oil
2 tsp. to 1 Tbsp. mugi or brown rice miso (see Glossary)
2 Tbsp. water
1 clove garlic, minced
½ tsp. powdered ginger
¼ tsp. basil
¼ tsp. marjoram
⅛ tsp. celery seed
pinch cayenne pepper
¼ cup chopped fresh parsley
⅔ cup tofu, mashed
Yield: 1 cup.

Combine all ingredients, except tofu, in a blender or food processor. With blender running, add mashed tofu, a little at a time, and blend until dressing is very smooth – about 1 minute. You may find that you need to add slightly more than 2 Tbsp. of water while blending in order to obtain a thick and creamy consistency.

Tofu Lemon Cream

This recipe is quickly prepared, and may be used with any dish that is usually accompanied by sour cream. Try it with Potato Kugel (p. 123), Spinach Chestnut Ring (p. 130), Tofu Latkes (p. 134), Burritos (p. 142), and with your favorite borscht recipe. For a more sour taste, cut down or eliminate the honey.

¼ cup lightly flavored oil	Blend or process all ingredients adding the tofu, piece by piece to the other ingredients. Chill before serving.
2 Tbsp. soymilk	
1 Tbsp. lemon juice	
½ to 1 tsp. honey	
⅛ tsp. salt	
8 oz. tofu	
Yield: 1½ cups.	

Tartar Sauce

This is a delicious companion to Pan-fried Tofu Sticks (p. 110), Baked Tofu Slices (p. 125) and Deep-fried Tofu Cutlets (p. 166).

1 cup Tofu Mayonnaise (p. 97)	Combine all ingredients in a bowl, and stir until smooth.
½ cup chopped dill pickle	
2 Tbsp. cider vinegar	
¾ tsp. curry powder	
¼ tsp. salt	
⅛ tsp. onion powder	
Yield: 1½ cups.	

Ginger Orange Sauce

Serve this sauce over grains, raw or lightly steamed vegetables.

1/2 cup orange juice concentrate
3 Tbsp. natural soy sauce or tamari
2 cloves garlic, pressed
1 Tbsp. freshly grated ginger
2 tsp. orange rind
8 oz. tofu
Yield: approximately 1¼ cups.

Blend all ingredients thoroughly in a food processor or blender, adding the tofu, piece by piece, to the other ingredients. The sauce should be at room temperature when served.

Tangy Dipping Sauce

We often serve this with Pan-fried Tofu Sticks (p. 110), but you may also wish to serve it with freshly made or chilled tofu.

1/4 cup water
2 Tbsp. catsup
2 tsp. natural soy sauce or tamari
2 tsp. Worcestershire sauce
1 tsp. horseradish
1/2 tsp. dry mustard
Yield: approximately 1/2 cup.

Combine all ingredients, taking care to blend the dry mustard thoroughly into the sauce.

Peanut Dipping Sauce

Try this dipping sauce with your freshly made tofu, or use it as a dipping sauce with Tempura (p. 172).

½ small onion, minced
3 Tbsp. natural soy sauce or tamari
3 Tbsp. lemon juice
2 Tbsp. peanut butter
2 Tbsp. brown sugar
2 cloves garlic, pressed
¼ tsp. crushed hot pepper
Yield: approximately 1½ cups.

Combine all ingredients in a blender, and whirl smooth.

Sesame Dipping Sauce

¼ cup sesame seeds
¼ cup natural soy sauce
¼ cup chicken or vegetable broth
1 Tbsp. sherry or sake
1 Tbsp. lemon juice
Yield: approximately 1 cup.

Toast the sesame seeds in a dry skillet over low to medium heat until they begin to pop. Move the pan back and forth, or stir gently to keep the seeds from sticking to the bottom of the pan.

Once toasted, grind the seeds in a blender. Add the remaining ingredients, and process until well blended.

Pour into a serving bowl or into individual dipping bowls.

Traditional Tempura Dipping Sauce

¾ cup chicken or vegetable broth
3 Tbsp. natural soy sauce or tamari
2 Tbsp. sherry or sake
4 Tbsp. grated white or red radish
3 Tbsp. grated fresh ginger root
horseradish, to taste (optional)
Yield: 1 cup.

Combine the broth, soy sauce and sherry in a small saucepan, and heat just to simmering, taking care that the mixture does not boil. Remove from heat, and cool to room temperature.

Place the grated radish and ginger root in a serving bowl, or distribute among individual dipping bowls. Pour in sauce.

Add horseradish to taste, or serve it separately.

Onion Sauce

This is a light-flavored, Béchamel-type sauce, sweet with the taste of onions. It can be used as a base for gratinées or with strongly flavored vegetables.

2 cups chopped onion	In a saucepan, sauté the onions until soft and golden in 4 Tbsp. of soy margarine with the ½ tsp. of salt. Set aside to cool.
6 to 8 Tbsp. soy margarine or butter	
½ tsp. salt	
1 cup soymilk	Blend together the soymilk and tofu, adding the tofu gradually to the soymilk. Add the sautéed onions, and purée until smooth. Return mixture to the saucepan.
8 oz. tofu	
½ cup white wine	
⅛ tsp. nutmeg	
salt to taste	Add the wine. Stirring constantly, cook for 5 minutes. Do not boil.
pinch pepper	
	Season with nutmeg, salt and pepper.
Yield: 3½ cups.	Just before serving, beat in 2 to 4 Tbsp. of soy margarine, a Tbsp. at a time.

Barbecue Sauce

The next time you are in the mood for outdoor cooking, try this tangy and full-bodied sauce with your favorite barbecue foods. Use one kind of miso or a combination. Each one will give you a slightly different flavor, from almost imperceptibly sweet and mellow (brown rice miso) to hearty, almost meaty (Hatcho) with mugi or barley miso filling in flavors in between. It keeps well, too.

We use this sauce as a marinade and basting sauce for tofu that has been pressed, frozen and then deep-fried.

¾ cup hot tap water	Pour the hot tap water into a blender or food processor. Add the miso and blend. When the miso-water mixture is smooth, add the remaining ingredients, and blend until smooth.
¼ cup miso	
8 oz. tomato sauce	
½ cup lemon juice	
1 Tbsp. + 1 tsp. prepared mustard	
1 tsp. Worcestershire sauce	
dash cayenne pepper	
few strips Jalapeño peppers (optional)	
Yield: 3 cups.	

Tomato Sauce

This sauce is meant as a basic Italian tomato sauce. You can add your own favorite ingredients. It makes a good base for a spaghetti sauce to which you can add, along with your favorite vegetables, sautéed or deep-fried tofu cubes (p. 167).

1 cup chopped onion	Sauté the onions and garlic in the olive oil for 5 minutes. If you are using mushrooms, add them now, and sauté for 5 more minutes.
2 cloves garlic, chopped	
¼ cup olive oil	
1½ cups sliced mushrooms (optional)	
2 28-oz. cans tomatoes, drained	Drain the tomatoes and add them to the onion mixture, breaking up the tomatoes with a spoon. Simmer uncovered for 30 minutes.
½ cup dry red wine	
1 Tbsp. basil	Add the wine, basil, salt, oregano and thyme, and simmer for 20 to 30 more minutes.
1½ tsp. salt	
1 tsp. oregano	
1 tsp. thyme	
Yield: approximately 5 cups.	

Sweet Poppy Dressing

This is an ideal dressing for fruits. Try it with Baked French Toast (p. 107) and your favorite fruit.

1 cup soymilk	Blend together the soymilk and tofu, adding the tofu gradually to the soymilk. Drizzle in the 3 to 4 Tbsp. of oil.
8 oz. tofu	
3 to 4 Tbsp. oil	
¼ cup honey	Add the honey, lemon juice, poppy seeds, and cinnamon.
¼ cup lemon juice	
2 Tbsp. poppy seeds	Chill, and use as a dressing for fruit salads.
1 tsp. cinnamon (optional)	
Yield: 2½ cups.	

Tomato Chutney

Once you prepare this chutney, which is only one of many combinations of fruits, vegetables and spices, you may find numerous uses for it beyond Curry Eggs and Tofu (p. 109). I also use it as a condiment with Deep-fried Tofu Cutlets (p. 166).

I have included a variation which calls for the substitution of honey and molasses for the traditional sugar. The chutney in this case is lighter and just slightly less sweet. Because of its relatively high acidity chutney should be cooked in stainless steel or enamel pans.

---

2 cups chopped, unpeeled tomatoes

1¼ cups pared and chopped tart apples

¾ cup chopped onion

¼ cup dark raisins

½ cup brown sugar, packed

¾ tsp. salt

¼ tsp. ginger

⅛ tsp. cayenne pepper

1 cup cider vinegar

Yield: 2 cups.

Combine all ingredients in a stainless steel or enamel saucepan. Heat to boiling. Reduce heat and simmer uncovered until thick, about 50 to 60 minutes. Stir occasionally.

Variation:
Substitute for brown sugar and 1 cup cider vinegar: 2 Tbsp. honey, ¼ cup molasses and ¾ cup cider vinegar. Proceed as above, although because of added liquid your cooking time will be between 20 to 30 minutes longer.

Entrées

This section features dishes which are substantial enough to be served as the main course of a meal, but includes others which may be used as accompaniments.

As in the rest of the book, the recipes have been loosely arranged according to the amount of cooking time required, beginning with those taking as little as 30 minutes to prepare and cook. I hasten to add that even among the best of cooks there can be variations in the amount of time it takes to prepare a certain dish. The arrangement here reflects an average arrived at by those developing and testing the recipes.

The recipes requiring marinating are grouped together on pages 161 to 164. Marinating adds, in most cases, considerable time to the preparation of a recipe, although not considerable additional effort. Do not feel that you must discard your marinades after you have used them once. Generally, the ingredients which make up a marinade will keep in the refrigerator indefinitely, and can be used again for the same dish or in a recipe of your own creation.

Our last section (pp. 165 to 174) is made up of recipes requiring deep-fried tofu. Before preparing any of these, you may wish to read or reread the section on deep-frying (p. 23), which – if done properly – will add non-greasy, delicious new varieties of cooked tofu to your repertoire.

Tofu Scrambled Eggs

This is a simple dish with a subtle taste of dark sesame oil, and is tasty just as it is or with the addition of your own favorite seasonings, such as fresh chives. While a serving of tofu scrambled eggs is as satisfying as regular scrambled eggs, those who have to watch their cholesterol intake will be happy to know that it contains only half an egg per serving. Dark sesame oil is also low in cholesterol. If you are preparing this for a meal to be served with other dishes, it should be one of the last dishes prepared, since it should not be cooked longer than 5 minutes. Scrambled tofu becomes rubbery if cooked too long, just as scrambled eggs do

1 lb. tofu	Press or squeeze the tofu (p. 22).
1 clove garlic, minced	Mince the garlic, and sauté in butter until light brown.
2 Tbsp. butter or margarine	
2 eggs, lightly beaten	Mash the tofu, and mix in the two lightly beaten eggs. Add the oil, salt, and pepper. Pour this mixture into the skillet with the garlic and butter. Cover, and cook over medium heat for 2 minutes. Then uncover, turn over the mixture and re-cover. Cook for 2 more minutes.
1 Tbsp. dark sesame oil	
½ tsp. salt	
dash freshly ground black pepper	
Yield: 4 servings.	Serve immediately.

Pancakes

2 cups whole wheat pastry or unbleached white flour	Combine the flour, baking soda, and salt in a mixing bowl.
1¾ tsp. baking soda	In a blender mix the water, oil, honey, and lemon juice. With the blender on, add the tofu, bit by bit, and blend until smooth.
½ tsp. salt	
1 cup water	
¼ cup oil or clarified butter	
1 Tbsp. honey	Beat the eggs slightly, then add to the liquid ingredients. Blend for 2 or 3 seconds.
1 Tbsp. lemon juice	
½ cup mashed tofu	Pour the liquid ingredients into the dry ingredients, and mix quickly. Do not overbeat or worry about lumps.
2 eggs	
	Cook a trial pancake to test the consistency of your batter. If the batter is too thick, add a small amount of water, by the spoonful. If it is too thin, add flour in the same way.
Yield: 6 to 8 servings.	

Baked French Toast

This is another of our favorite recipes which we usually serve with fresh or cooked fruit (try fresh strawberries or cooked pears) and Sweet Poppy Dressing (p. 103) at breakfast or brunch. This dish is sweet enough that no other sweetener is required, although I am told it's very good with maple syrup.

6 eggs	Preheat oven to 350°.
1 lb. tofu	In a food processor or blender, purée all ingredients, except the buttered bread and nutmeg, adding the tofu gradually to the other ingredients.
½ cup honey	
1 tsp. vanilla	
1 tsp. lemon rind	
1 to 2 tsp. lemon juice (optional)	Line the bottom of a 9 × 13-inch baking dish with the bread. Pour the tofu mixture over the bread. Sprinkle lightly with nutmeg.
½ tsp. cinnamon	
⅛ tsp. salt	
6 pieces whole wheat or raisin bread, buttered on both sides	Bake at 350° for 20 to 30 minutes or until the custard has set.
nutmeg	Serve warm.
Yield: 5 to 6 servings.	

Waffles

1¾ cups all-purpose or whole wheat pastry flour

3 tsp. baking powder

½ tsp. salt

⅛ tsp. nutmeg

3 eggs

¾ cup mashed tofu

¾ cup water

1½ Tbsp. honey

1½ tsp. vanilla

⅓ cup melted butter or soy margarine

Combine the dry ingredients in a bowl. Blend together the remaining ingredients – eggs, tofu, water, honey, vanilla and butter – until very smooth. Add the liquid to the dry ingredients and stir only until they are thoroughly moistened.

Bake on a heated waffle iron.

Variations:

Orange Bran Waffles
Substitute ¾ cup bran cereal for ¾ cup of the flour. Add the grated rind of 1 medium orange to the liquid ingredients. Proceed as in the basic recipe.

Banana Walnut Waffles
Add 1 cup of chopped walnuts to the dry ingredients. Blend 1 medium banana, peeled and cut into pieces, with the liquid ingredients.

Apple Spice Waffles
Instead of ⅛ tsp. nutmeg, add ¾ tsp. ground cinnamon and ¼ tsp. ground nutmeg to the dry ingredients. Stir in the liquid and add 1 medium apple, pared and grated.

Carob Waffles
Substitute ½ cup carob powder for ½ cup of the flour. Add the liquid to the dry ingredients and stir in ½ cup finely chopped raisins or dates. Serve with fresh strawberries and whipped cream.

Yield: 4 to 6 waffles.

Curry Eggs and Tofu with Chutney

As an entrée at brunch or an after-theater repast, this is most elegant. And if you already have chutney on hand, it can be prepared very quickly as well. If you do not have whipping cream or cannot eat it, try the variation below for a slightly more delicate, but equally delicious taste.

½ cup Tomato Chutney (p. 104) or any prepared chutney
8 oz. tofu
4 eggs
½ cup whipping cream
¾ tsp. curry powder
⅛ tsp. salt
crystallized ginger (optional)

Prepare the Tomato Chutney. When it has nearly finished cooking, preheat the oven to 375° and proceed with the remainder of the recipe. If you are using a prepared chutney, heat it up. Place 2 tablespoons in each of 4 buttered custard cups.

Cut 4 rounds of tofu ⅜ to ½-inch thick, to fit into the custard cups. Place on top of the chutney.

Break an egg into a separate bowl, then slide it into one of the custard cups on top of the tofu. Repeat the same procedure with each of the three remaining eggs.

Place the custard cups into a dish of water – a 9 × 9-inch cake pan works well. Bake until the eggs have set, about 15 to 20 minutes.

Meanwhile bring the cream, curry powder and salt to boil in a small saucepan. Immediately lower the heat and simmer for 5 minutes until thickened. Garnish the cooked eggs with the curry sauce and chopped crystallized ginger.

Variation:
For a lighter curry sauce, substitute for the whipping cream ½ cup and 1 Tbsp. soymilk plus 1 tsp. arrowroot, cornstarch or kudzu.

Dissolve the arrowroot in 1 Tbsp. of soymilk. Heat the remaining ½ cup of soymilk, but do not boil. Re-stir the arrowroot-soymilk solution and then add it to the heating soymilk. Stir until thickened, about 5 minutes. Remove from heat and use as above.

Yield: 4 servings.

Steamed Tofu with Peas and Mushrooms

2 lb. tofu
3½ cups sliced mushrooms
1 cup peas
1½ to 2 Tbsp. oil
½ cup natural soy sauce or tamari

Yield: 4 to 6 servings.

Press the tofu for 20 to 30 minutes (p. 22). Slice the mushrooms and sauté them in the oil until done, about 10 minutes.

Cook the peas. Cut the tofu into ¾-inch cubes, and steam over boiling water for 5 minutes until heated through. When done, gently mix with the mushrooms, peas, and soy sauce in a pre-heated serving bowl or casserole.

Serve immediately with rice.

Pan-fried Tofu Sticks

These can be very quickly prepared, within 20 to 30 minutes, and may be served alone with the Tangy Dipping Sauce (p. 100), or in a bun with crisp lettuce, sprouts and the dipping sauce.

¼ cup cornmeal
1 Tbsp. nutritional yeast
2 Tbsp. wheat germ
⅛ tsp. garlic powder
⅛ tsp. curry powder
⅛ tsp. thyme
dash cayenne pepper
dash salt
1 lb. tofu
2 Tbsp. oil
Yield: 4 servings.

Combine all the dry ingredients in a shallow bowl and mix well. Cut the tofu into 4 × 1 × ½-inch strips.

Dredge the tofu thoroughly in the corn-meal mixture, and fry in the oil on all sides until crispy and golden brown.

Spicy Braised Bean Curd

Are you in a hurry? This recipe can be quickly prepared, but it won't taste like fast food.

1 lb. tofu	Cut the tofu into 1-inch cubes, and sauté them in the sesame oil until a golden crust forms on all sides. Set aside.
2 Tbsp. sesame oil	
SAUCE:	
¼ cup natural soy sauce	In a saucepan, combine the soy sauce, brown sugar, vinegar, garlic powder, mustard, and water, and heat to a simmer.
3 Tbsp. brown sugar	
3 Tbsp. vinegar	
¾ tsp. garlic powder	Meanwhile, dissolve the arrowroot in 2 Tbsp. of water. Add to the simmering sauce, whisking to mix thoroughly. Cook until thick.
¼ tsp. dry mustard	
½ cup water	
1 Tbsp. arrowroot, cornstarch, or kudzu	Add the thickened sauce to the sautéed tofu in the frying pan, and simmer gently for 8 to 10 minutes.
2 Tbsp. water	
⅓ cup chopped scallions, for garnish	Serve hot, garnish with the chopped scallions and, if desired, the grated ginger root.
1 Tbsp. grated fresh ginger root (optional)	
Yield: 3 to 4 servings.	

Tofu in Tahini Sauce

Serve this dish with assorted fresh vegetables, salad greens and rice. You can be eating in 30 minutes, and getting essential nutrients, too. This is an excellent dish to serve when surprised by guests for dinner.

2 lb. tofu	Cut the tofu cakes into pieces approximately 4 × 4 × 1 inch. Set aside.
SAUCE:	Sauté the onion in the oil until soft. Mix together the remaining ingredients, except the scallions, and add to the onions. Heat and stir over low heat until thick.
⅓ cup finely chopped onion	
1 Tbsp. dark sesame oil	
1 cup tahini	
1¼ cups water	Steam the tofu pieces for five minutes, or parboil them (p. 21) to thoroughly warm them. Then place them in a preheated casserole or 9 × 13-inch baking dish. Pour the hot sauce over them, garnish with chopped scallions, and serve immediately.
2 Tbsp. natural soy sauce or tamari	
⅛ tsp. mace	
chopped scallions as garnish	
Yield: 4 servings.	

Zucchini Onion Barbecue

Frozen tofu is the natural food answer to on-the-table-quick dinners. It's always good to have some on hand. This dinner can be made within 30 minutes.

8 to 12 oz. frozen tofu	
1 to 1½ cups Barbecue Sauce (p. 102 or 115) or a prepared tomato or barbecue sauce	
1 medium onion, finely chopped	
2 cloves garlic, pressed (optional)	
2 Tbsp. oil or butter	
1 medium zucchini, sliced	
1½ cups chopped mushrooms	

Thaw out the frozen tofu (p. 19), then crumble, shred, or finely chop it, and put it into the barbecue sauce to marinate.

While the tofu is marinating, sauté the chopped onions and garlic in oil or butter until clear. Add the zucchini and mushrooms and cook until tender. At this point, add the tofu with the sauce. Add more barbecue sauce if you wish.

Cook until the tofu is warmed through. To preserve the great nutritional value of the miso in the barbecue sauce, it is best not to boil the mixture.

Yield: 4 servings.

Serve with your favorite grain or noodles, or topped with grated cheese.

Eggplant Casserole

8 oz. tofu

1 medium onion, chopped

1 to 2 Tbsp. oil

1 medium eggplant, peeled and cubed

1 16-oz. can stewed tomatoes

1 Tbsp. sherry or sake

½ tsp. marjoram

¼ tsp. rosemary

salt and pepper to taste

4 oz. Parmesan cheese

Cut the tofu into ½-inch cubes.

Sauté the chopped onion in 1 Tbsp. of oil until almost done. Add the cubed eggplant, and sauté for a few minutes until browned, adding an additional Tbsp. of oil, if necessary, to prevent sticking.

Add the cubed tofu, the stewed tomatoes, sherry, marjoram and rosemary. Simmer until the eggplant is tender. Salt and pepper to taste. Serve with grated Parmesan cheese.

Variation 1:
Preheat oven to 375°. Proceed as above until eggplant is tender. Then transfer the mixture to a casserole. Top with 4 oz. American cheese, sliced or grated. Bake until cheese melts.

Variation 2:
Preheat oven to 375°. Proceed as above until eggplant is tender. Then transfer the mixture to a casserole. Mix in ½ cup cottage cheese. Top with 4 oz. grated Parmesan or grated or sliced American cheese, and bake in oven until the mixture is heated through and the cheese melts.

Yield: 4 servings.

Tofu in Sweet and Sour Mushroom Sauce

This sauce is not unlike the translucent sauces used so often in Chinese cooking. In the winter, served with rice and a salad, it makes a hearty, satisfying meal. In the summer, try it with salad.

2 lb. tofu

SAUCE:

1 small onion

1 small green pepper (or ½ medium)

1 to 2 Tbsp. oil (sesame or sunflower, preferably)

1 medium clove garlic, pressed

1½ to 2 cups sliced fresh mushrooms

2 to 3 Tbsp. arrowroot, cornstarch or kudzu

1 cup water

¼ tsp thyme

¼ tsp. basil

⅛ tsp. powdered ginger (optional)

2 Tbsp. cider vinegar

1 to 2 Tbsp. honey

freshly ground black pepper, to taste

chopped dried chili peppers, to taste (optional)

2 Tbsp. Dijon mustard

2 to 3 Tbsp. natural soy sauce or tamari

3 to 5 scallions, chopped, for garnish

Yield: 6 servings

Chop the onion and green pepper into small pieces, and put into a saucepan with the oil. Add the garlic, and sauté for 3 minutes. Add the chopped mushrooms, and cover. Cook over low heat, stirring occasionally to prevent sticking, until the onions are translucent and the mushrooms tender.

Mix the arrowroot with ½ cup of water, and stir with a fork until thoroughly dissolved. Add the thyme, basil, ginger and vinegar to the solution, and stir again. Pour this mixture into the saucepan with the vegetables, then quickly pour in the remaining ½ cup of water.

Stir the mixture over low to medium heat until it starts to thicken. Then lower the heat, and simmer. Stir in the honey, pepper, and small amount of chopped chili peppers, if you want a hot sweet and sour sauce. Stir in the mustard, and finally the soy sauce.

(If the sauce seems too thick, add water a little bit at a time. If it is too thin, dissolve ½ to 1 Tbsp. of arrowroot in 2 Tbsp. of water, add to the sauce, and heat a few minutes more.)

At this point, the heat can be turned off and the sauce reheated later, if necessary. It is a good idea for it to sit for 10 to 15 minutes to allow the flavors to blend. If necessary, reheat just before pouring over the steamed tofu.

Cut the tofu cakes into ¾ to 1-inch cubes and steam for 5 minutes. Let them drain slightly, then place them in a 9 × 13-inch pre-heated baking dish. Cover with the sauce and garnish with chopped scallions. Serve immediately.

Vegetable Pie

2 cups chopped broccoli
or cauliflower

¹/₂ cup finely chopped onion

¹/₂ cup finely chopped
green pepper

1¹/₂ cups grated Cheddar cheese

³/₄ cup mashed tofu

¹/₂ cup water

¹/₂ cup whole wheat or
unbleached white flour
(or half and half)

¹/₂ tsp. baking powder

¹/₄ tsp. garlic powder

¹/₄ to ¹/₂ tsp. salt

¹/₄ tsp. pepper

Yield: 4 to 6 servings.

Preheat the oven to 400°.

Grease a 10 × 1¹/₂-inch pie plate.

Partially cook the broccoli or cauliflower in a steamer or in boiling salted water for 2 to 3 minutes. Drain.

Mix together the broccoli or cauliflower in the pie plate with the chopped onions, peppers, and 1 cup grated cheese.

In a blender or food processor, combine the tofu, water, flour, the remaining ¹/₂ cup cheese, and seasonings. Blend until smooth. Pour this mixture over the cheese and vegetables in the pie plate.

Bake for 35 to 40 minutes until golden brown and knife inserted comes out clean. If you wish, brush melted butter on the top during the last 5 minutes of baking.

Oven-Cooked Barbecue Tofu

1¹/₂ lb. tofu

SAUCE:

1 small onion, chopped

1 Tbsp. oil

2 Tbsp. vinegar

1 Tbsp. Worcestershire sauce

2 Tbsp. molasses

5 Tbsp. natural soy sauce
or tamari

1 cup Tomato Sauce (p. 103)

Yield: 3 to 4 servings.

To prepare the sauce, sauté the chopped onion in the oil until golden. Add the vinegar, Worcestershire sauce, molasses, soy sauce, and tomato sauce. Simmer for 10 minutes.

Oil a shallow-sided cookie sheet or circular pizza pan. Then brush a small amount of marinade on the bottom of the pan. Cut each cake of tofu into eight strips. Lay these on the pan. Then pour the sauce over the tofu strips, making sure that the top of each strip is well-covered. Marinate for 30 minutes.

Preheat the oven to 350°.

Before baking, brush the strips with the sauce or spoon it on again.

Bake for 30 to 40 minutes until the sauce has dried out and sticks to the tofu.

Serve hot or cold.

Baked Tofu Mozzarella

This delightful entrée from the Regular Restaurant in Rochester, New York, can be prepared in less than an hour. Enjoy it with garlic bread and a tossed salad.

1½ lb. tofu

1 cup whole wheat bread crumbs

½ Tbsp. basil

½ Tbsp. oregano

2 eggs

1 Tbsp. natural soy sauce or tamari

2 cloves garlic, minced, or ¼ tsp. garlic powder

flour for dredging

2 cups Tomato Sauce (p. 103), or commercially prepared tomato sauce

sautéed mushrooms or chopped black olives (optional)

8 oz. grated Mozzarella cheese

Yield: 4 to 6 servings.

Press the tofu for 30 minutes (p. 22).

Preheat oven to 375°.

In a small bowl, combine the bread crumbs, basil, and oregano. In another small bowl, beat the eggs with the soy sauce and garlic.

Pat the tofu dry with paper towels. Cut each cake into four triangles. Dredge each triangle in flour, then dip it in the egg mixture and then into the bread crumbs. Place the coated triangles on a baking sheet. Bake at 375° for 20 minutes, until golden and crisp.

Remove from oven and place tofu triangles in a greased casserole dish. Cover with tomato sauce, sautéed mushrooms or chopped black olives and grated Mozzarella cheese. Bake again just until cheese melts, then serve.

Enchilada Casserole

There are times when many of us want a spicy meal with special ingredients, but we just can't spare the time to prepare everything from scratch. These are the times when we can be grateful for the convenience of canned and prepared foods. This recipe, a gift from a busy professional woman and excellent cook, makes optimal use of them.

1 lb. tofu
1 small onion, chopped
1 clove garlic, pressed
2 Tbsp. oil
1 16-oz. can peeled tomatoes
1 to 1½ tsp. salt, to taste
½ to 1 tsp. cumin, to taste
1 4-oz. can chopped green chili peppers
1 16-oz. can enchilada sauce
1 16-oz. can kidney beans
1 egg, beaten
8 to 10 oz. grated Cheddar or Jack cheese
1 to 3 tsp. chili powder, to taste
12 corn tortillas
chopped scallions or chives as garnish.

Squeeze tofu well, or press for 30 to 60 minutes (p. 22).

Preheat oven to 350°.

Sauté the onion and garlic in the oil for 5 minutes. Meanwhile mash the tomatoes or purée them in a blender. Then add them along with ½ to 1 tsp. salt, ½ tsp. cumin, ½ of the can of green chili peppers and the enchilada sauce to the onion and garlic. Allow to simmer while you prepare the filling.

Drain and mash the kidney beans. Add the tofu and mash it into the beans so that the two are thoroughly mixed. Add the egg, the remaining half of the chili peppers, half of the shredded cheese, the chili powder and the remaining salt.

Cover the bottom of a 9 × 13-inch baking pan with one-third of the sauce.

Spread one side of each of the tortillas with sauce. Brushing on the sauce with a pastry brush works very nicely so that there is a thin coating of sauce on the inside of the tortilla before you put on the filling. Divide the filling equally among the tortillas. Put the filling on the coated side of the tortilla. Roll up the tortillas and place them seam-side down in the baking pan. Pour the remaining sauce over the top.

Bake for 25 to 30 minutes until the sauce is bubbly. Top with the remaining cheese 5 minutes before removing from the oven.

If desired, serve with rice and top with chopped scallions or chives.

Yield: 4 to 6 servings.

Make-Ahead-and-Freeze Cheese Soufflé

This recipe requires a short preparation time whether you wish to serve it right away or make it ahead of time, then freeze it and cook it later. One of the keys to its success is stirring well at each stage to insure that the mixture is smooth; another is gently folding in the egg whites which are stiff, but not dry. As a variation, try the soufflé with the addition of finely chopped broccoli.

½ cup butter or soy margarine
¾ cup unbleached all-purpose flour
½ to 1 tsp. salt
¼ tsp. dry mustard
⅛ tsp. onion powder
¾ cup mashed tofu
¾ cup water
1½ cups grated Cheddar cheese
¼ tsp. Worcestershire sauce
6 eggs, at room temperature

If you plan to cook the soufflé immediately after making it, rather than freeze it, set the cooking rack in your oven just below the center line of the oven, and preheat to 350°.

Butter the bottom and sides of a (preferably straight-sided) 2-quart soufflé dish or casserole, then dust with flour. (This will allow the soufflé to climb higher during cooking, as well as prevent the delicious thick crust from sticking to the sides of the dish.)

Melt the butter or soy margarine in a saucepan, then stir in the flour, salt, dry mustard, and onion powder. Cook over low heat for 2 minutes, stirring constantly. Remove from heat.

Blend the tofu and water until smooth; then add to the mixture in the saucepan. Stir and cook until thick and smooth.

Stir in the grated Cheddar cheese. Continue to stir over low heat until very smooth. Remove from heat, and stir in the Worcestershire sauce until well-blended. Allow the mixture to cool slightly.

Separate the eggs, setting the whites aside. Once the soufflé mixture has cooled, blend the egg yolks into it, one at a time.

Beat the egg whites until stiff, but not dry. Fold them gently into the soufflé mixture. Pour the mixture into the soufflé dish or casserole. Bake for 45 to 55 minutes, or until set, without peeking into the oven until very near the end of the cooking time. Serve immediately.

If you wish to freeze the soufflé, after gently folding in the egg whites, pour the mixture immediately into the soufflé dish or casserole, buttered and dusted as above. Cover the dish tightly with foil, and place immediately in the freezer.

To bake from its frozen state, remove the foil and bake in a preheated 350° oven for 1 to 1¼ hours. Serve immediately.

Variation:
Parboil ¾ cup finely chopped fresh broccoli for 2 to 3 minutes, then immediately plunge the broccoli into cold water. Drain and pat dry. (Or ¾ cup finely chopped frozen broccoli, thawed to room temperature, drained and patted dry.)

Add the broccoli before adding the egg yolks; proceed as above.

Yield: 6 to 8 servings.

Ginger Garlic Tofu

If you wish to prepare this dish ahead of time, you can cook the sauce, pour it into a baking dish with the tofu slices, and allow them to marinate for 1 to 2 hours before baking. Prepare the garnishes just before the dish comes out of the oven, so that you can add them quickly, and serve immediately.

While it is usually served with rice, it is also delicious served over thin rice noodles.

2 lb. tofu

½ cup safflower oil

2 Tbsp. dark sesame oil

2½ cups finely chopped onions

4 large cloves garlic, pressed

3 Tbsp. grated fresh ginger

2 Tbsp. arrowroot, cornstarch or kudzu

1½ cups cool water or light vegetable stock

⅓ cup natural soy sauce

2 Tbsp. wine vinegar

1 Tbsp. honey

⅔ cup thinly sliced scallions

2 Tbsp. roasted sesame seeds

Preheat oven to 350°.

Cut tofu into ½ × 3 × 2-inch slices and press for 15 minutes (p. 22).

Heat both oils in a large, heavy saucepan and sauté onions and garlic until translucent. Add grated ginger and cook for 5 minutes longer. Dissolve the arrowroot in the water, then add it to the onions along with the soy sauce, vinegar and honey. Bring sauce to a boil over high heat, stirring constantly. Reduce heat and simmer for 5 to 7 minutes, or until sauce has thickened.

Pour a thin layer of sauce in the bottom of an 8 × 12-inch baking pan. Arrange half of the tofu slices in the dish, followed by a thin layer of sauce, a second layer of tofu, and a final layer of sauce.

Bake for 20 to 25 minutes or until heated through and bubbling.

Garnish with chopped scallions and roasted sesame seeds.

Serve immediately.

Variation:
For a festive variation, arrange 1 cup seeded and halved grapes, cut-side down, between the second layer of tofu and the final layer of sauce.

Bake as directed above, and garnish with sesame seeds and 4 or 5 paper-thin orange slices to replace the chopped scallions.

Yield: 6 to 8 servings.

Baked Tofu with Cheese and Wine

Do you have company coming soon, and not much time to prepare a meal? Give this recipe a try. It makes a very elegant dinner served with steamed broccoli in lemon-butter sauce, a green salad with vinaigrette dressing and your favorite dessert.

2 medium onions, finely chopped

4 cloves garlic, pressed

3 Tbsp. oil

1 heaping Tbsp. butter

2 cups chopped mushrooms

½ tsp. salt

½ tsp. thyme

2 lb. tofu, pressed

6 oz. Monterey Jack or mild Cheddar cheese

½ cup Rhine wine

1 Tbsp. Worcestershire sauce

1 Tbsp. sesame seeds

¼ cup chopped scallion greens or tops

Yield: 4 to 6 servings.

Preheat oven to 350°.

In a large skillet, sauté the chopped onions and pressed garlic in the oil and butter. When the onions are clear and translucent, add the mushrooms and salt. Continue to sauté for 10 minutes. During the last 5 minutes, add the thyme.

Cut the pressed tofu into ½-inch cubes. Grate the cheese.

Oil a 2-quart casserole dish.

Lay half the tofu cubes in the bottom of the casserole dish. Follow this with a layer of sautéed onions and mushrooms and a layer of grated cheese. Start again with a layer of the remaining tofu, followed by the rest of the sautéed onions and mushrooms, and end with all but 2 to 3 Tbsp. of the grated cheese.

Pour the wine and Worcestershire sauce into the casserole, and mix gently. Sprinkle the remaining cheese on top, and then the sesame seeds.

Bake uncovered for 20 minutes to warm tofu and melt the cheese. Just before serving, sprinkle the chopped scallion greens on the top.

Spicy Tofu and Eggplant in Black Bean Sauce

This recipe will give you an opportunity to enjoy tofu in a more traditional manner, since it is an adaptation of a dish from Chungking in mainland China. Salted black beans and Szechuan peppercorn powder may be purchased from oriental food markets.

small eggplant, peeled
salt
8 to 12 oz. tofu
3 to 4 Tbsp. oil
1 Tbsp. minced scallions
1 tsp. minced garlic
1/2 tsp. cayenne powder (or more, to taste)
2 to 3 Tbsp. mashed salted black beans (or more, to taste)
1 Tbsp. natural soy sauce or tamari
1/2 cup vegetable or chicken stock
2 tsp. arrowroot, cornstarch or kudzu
2 Tbsp. water
Szechuan peppercorn powder (optional)

Wash the eggplant. Cut it into 1/2-inch cubes to make 1 cup. Salt the cubes, and leave them to drain for 15 minutes.

Cut the tofu into 1/2 inch cubes.

Pat the eggplant cubes dry in paper towels. Heat the oil in a frying pan or wok. Stir-fry the eggplant over high heat until soft. Add more oil if needed to prevent sticking and burning. Remove eggplant from pan and set aside.

In the same pan, stir-fry the minced scallions, minced garlic, and cayenne powder for 1 to 2 minutes, until the flavors are released. Add more oil if needed. Add the salted black beans, natural soy sauce and stock.

Gently stir in the tofu and eggplant cubes. Taste and adjust seasonings (i.e., add more black beans, cayenne powder and/or salt). Cover pan, and cook over low heat for 15 minutes, stirring occasionally.

Dissolve the arrowroot in water, pour into the eggplant-tofu mixture, and stir gently until the sauce thickens. Transfer the mixture into a serving dish, sprinkle with Szechuan peppercorn powder, if you wish, and serve immediately.

Yield: 2 to 3 servings

Potato Kugel

The preparation time is short, and the dish is hearty, good for a simple meal on a cold day.

2 lb. potatoes, washed and grated coarsely

1 large onion, finely chopped

1 cup mashed tofu

1½ tsp. salt

¼ tsp. black pepper

3 eggs

3 Tbsp. oil

Yield: 6 servings.

Preheat oven to 350°.

Combine the potatoes, onions and tofu. Mix the salt, pepper, and eggs into the potato mixture.

Pour the oil into a 9 × 13-inch baking dish, and put it into the oven for a few minutes just to heat the oil. After the oil is heated, turn the potato mixture into the baking dish. Bake 60 to 70 minutes until the mixture is crusty on top. Serve with Tofu Lemon Cream (p. 99) or sour cream.

Stir-fried Tofu Dumplings with Vegetables

This is a somewhat westernized version of a Chinese dish from Shanghai. In this case, if you are able to locate the Chinese-style firm tofu, so much the better. But the Japanese-style regular or medium-firm tofu also works nicely, although it should be pressed under a 5- to 10-lb. weight for 30 to 60 minutes before using. This is a dish in which vegetable substitutions may be easily made.

12 oz. firm tofu, or 1 lb. regular tofu, pressed (p.22)

1/2 tsp. flour

1/4 tsp. salt

oil for deep-frying

1 small carrot, thinly sliced

1 1/2 cups sliced mushrooms

8 oz. spinach, with stems removed and cut into 2-inch pieces (or 4 oz. bok choy or Chinese cabbage, chopped)

1 1/2 Tbsp. natural soy sauce or tamari

1 tsp. sherry or sake

1 tsp. honey

1 cup chicken or vegetable stock

2 tsp. arrowroot, cornstarch, or kudzu

2 Tbsp. water

Yield: 2 to 3 servings.

Mash the tofu in a small bowl with a fork. Mix in the flour and salt. Form the mixture into small balls about 2/3-inch in diameter.

Pour enough oil into a heavy-gauge, deep-sided pot, a deep-fryer or wok to bring it to a height of 2 inches in the pot. Heat the oil to 350° to 375°. Deep-fry the tofu dumplings until golden brown, then drain on paper towels.

In a frying pan, heat 1 Tbsp. of oil, and stir-fry the sliced carrot and mushrooms for 2 to 3 minutes until crisp-tender, adding the spinach in the last 30 seconds.

Add the soy sauce, sherry or sake, honey and stock, and bring to a boil. Meanwhile, dissolve the arrowroot in the 2 Tbsp. of water.

Once the sauce has boiled, reduce the heat, and add the arrowroot solution. Add the tofu dumplings, and heat through. Serve with rice.

If you have any dark sesame oil (available in Oriental food stores or supermarket sections), try sprinkling a few drops over your serving.

Baked Tofu Slices with Tartar Sauce

These make an excellent meal served with steamed and buttered green beans and a tossed salad or coleslaw.

1½ lb. tofu
1 cup whole wheat flour
2 eggs, beaten
1 Tbsp. natural soy sauce or tamari
⅔ cup finely ground cornmeal
¼ tsp. garlic powder
¼ tsp. dry mustard
¼ tsp. salt
⅛ tsp. curry powder
Tartar Sauce (p. 99)
lemon wedges, as garnish

Preheat oven to 350°.

Oil or grease a cookie sheet thoroughly.

Cut the tofu cakes into quarters.

Prepare the dredging mixtures. Have the whole wheat flour nearby; in a separate bowl mix together the beaten eggs and soy sauce; in another bowl, combine the cornmeal, garlic powder, dry mustard, salt and curry powder. (Since dredging is a messy business, at best, it is advisable not to put the complete amounts of the whole wheat flour or the other two mixtures into the three bowls at once, but rather to add the mixtures as needed. In this way, smaller amounts of the dredging materials will be wasted.)

First dredge the tofu slices in whole wheat flour; then dip them in the egg-soy sauce mixture, and finally dredge them in the cornmeal mixture.

Place the tofu on the cookie sheet. Brush the tops lightly with oil. Bake 10 minutes per side until well-browned.

Serve with lemon wedges and tartar sauce.

Yield: 4 servings

Tomato Basil Cheese Pie

CRUST:

1 cup whole wheat pastry or unbleached white flour or a mixture
1 Tbsp. nutritional yeast
1/2 tsp. salt
1/3 cup oil or clarified butter
1 1/2 Tbsp. cold soymilk or dairy milk
1/2 tsp. lemon juice

FILLING:

8 oz. tofu
3/4 cup water
1/2 tsp. salt
1/8 tsp. cumin
1/8 tsp. oregano
1/8 tsp. garlic powder
1/8 tsp. onion powder
dash pepper
1 1/4 cup grated Swiss, Gruyère or mild cheese
1 Tbsp. flour
2 Tbsp. olive oil
1 medium onion, thinly sliced
2 medium ripe, firm tomatoes, sliced (no more than 2 cups)
1 1/2 Tbsp. chopped fresh basil, or 1 tsp. dried basil
2 small eggs

Yield: 4 to 5 servings.

Preheat oven to 475°.

To prepare the crust, sift together the flour, yeast, and salt.

Combine the oil and soymilk; whisk together until smooth and creamy. Continue stirring as you add the lemon juice.

Pour the oil-soymilk mixture over the dry ingredients; mix together lightly with a fork. Turn into a deep 9 or 9 1/2-inch pie pan.

Pat the dough into a crust using your fingers or the back of a spoon, taking care not to handle the dough any more than necessary. When you have finished, prick the dough with a fork, then bake in a 475° oven for 12 to 15 minutes. Allow the oven to cool to 350°.

Combine the tofu, water, and seasonings in a blender until smooth. Add 1/4 cup of the grated cheese to the tofu mixture in the blender. Set aside.

Mix the flour with the remaining cup of grated cheese. After the pie crust has cooled, sprinkle 1/2 cup of cheese on the bottom of the crust.

Heat the olive oil, then sauté the onions until soft and translucent. Arrange the cooked onions on top of the layer of cheese. Using the same frying pan, cook the tomatoes with the basil for 2 minutes. If necessary add more oil. Arrange the tomatoes on top of the onions, and then top with the remaining 1/2 cup of cheese.

Return to the mixture in the blender. Drop in the two eggs, and blend for no more than 30 seconds. Pour this mixture over the rest of the filling ingredients.

Bake at 350° for 45 minutes to 1 hour, or until a knife inserted in the center comes out clean.

Baked Frittata

The frittata is a highly versatile meal in one pan, which can be put together quite easily, if you don't mind a bit of chopping, dicing and mincing. This dish, inspired by Rochester's Regular Restaurant, provides an excellent opportunity for using up any surplus vegetables you might have on hand.

8 oz. tofu
1 large onion, diced
1 green pepper, diced
1 small zucchini, diced
1 stalk celery, diced
1 medium carrot, diced
2 cloves garlic, minced
3 to 4 Tbsp. olive or safflower oil
1½ tsp. oregano
1 tsp. basil
¾ tsp. salt
black pepper, freshly ground
1 small tomato, chopped
3 eggs

Press or squeeze the tofu (p. 22) and preheat the oven to 400°.

In a large skillet or casserole which can be used over direct heat and in the oven, sauté the diced onion, green pepper, zucchini, celery, carrot and minced garlic in the oil. Season the mixture with oregano, basil, salt, and black pepper.

Add the chopped tomato. Taste and adjust seasonings. Then remove from the heat. Break the tofu into small pieces and put in a blender or food processor. Drop in the 3 eggs and blend briefly. Add the egg-tofu mixture to the sautéed vegetables and stir it in well.

Place the skillet or casserole in the oven and bake for 20 to 30 minutes until set and slightly puffed.

Serve as is or with a light tomato sauce, grated Cheddar or Parmesan cheese. If you wish to add cheese, try sprinkling it on during the last 5 minutes of baking.

Variations:
By varying the seasonings and vegetables used you can highlight different cuisines. In each case you will want to use from 3½ to 4 cups of vegetables.

Mexican: cumin, garlic, oregano, cayenne, onion, green peppers, chili peppers, tomatoes.

Slavic: caraway seed, dried mustard, cabbage, onion.

Mediterranean: fresh basil, garlic, onions, zucchini, tomatoes, eggplant.

Yield: 4 to 6 servings.

Puffed Tofu Cheese Cornbread

This hearty dish from the Regular Restaurant is an ideal choice for a meal on cold winter days.

CORNBREAD:

½ cup whole wheat pastry or unbleached white flour (or a mixture)

½ cup cornmeal

1 tsp. baking powder

¼ tsp. baking soda

½ tsp. salt

1 egg

½ cup soymilk or dairy milk

1 Tbsp. honey

2 tsp. cider vinegar

TOFU-CHEESE-EGG MIX:

1¼ cups grated sharp Cheddar cheese

2 Tbsp. chopped onion

8 to 10 oz. tofu, cut in 4 × 4 × ½-inch slices

1¼ cups soymilk or dairy milk

2 Tbsp. barley miso (see Glossary)

2 Tbsp. prepared mustard

dash pepper

3 eggs

paprika, as garnish

Yield: 4 to 6 servings.

Preheat oven to 350°.

Oil a 2-quart casserole or soufflé dish, and dust lightly with flour.

Begin by preparing the cornbread. Sift together the flour, cornmeal, baking powder, baking soda, and salt. Then beat together the egg, soymilk, and honey. Add the wet ingredients to the dry, and stir until just mixed, taking care not to overstir. Finally, quickly stir in the vinegar, then pour into the casserole or soufflé dish, and immediately put into the oven. Bake for 10 minutes, or until the cornbread batter is set.

Remove the cornbread from the oven, and poke through the surface in a dozen places with a knife. Layer the grated cheese, onions, and tofu on top of the cornbread.

Combine the soymilk, miso, mustard, and pepper in a blender, and blend until the miso is well mixed. Add the eggs, and blend for 10 seconds. Pour into the casserole; then sprinkle paprika over the top.

Bake for 45 minutes, or until set.

Curried Tofu with Broccoli

8 oz. tofu	Preheat oven to 350°.
2 tsp. sesame oil	Cut the cake of tofu into ¼-inch thick slices. Place in a pan, cover, and braise them lightly in the sesame oil until golden. Set aside.
12 oz. broccoli, with tough outer skin removed from the stalks	

CURRY SAUCE:

1 cup soymilk

1 Tbsp. curry

3 Tbsp. vinegar

¼ cup corn oil

8 oz. tofu

Preheat oven to 350°.

Cut the cake of tofu into ¼-inch thick slices. Place in a pan, cover, and braise them lightly in the sesame oil until golden. Set aside.

Steam the broccoli until just tender.

In a blender or food processor, thoroughly mix all the curry sauce ingredients, adding the tofu gradually to the other ingredients.

Oil a 1½-quart casserole with sesame oil.

Mix one-half of the sauce with the braised tofu. Put a layer of braised tofu and sauce mixture on the bottom of the casserole.

Add a layer of broccoli and one-half of the remaining sauce.

Add the remaining braised tofu-sauce mix, and finish off with a layer of broccoli and the rest of the curry sauce.

Cover, and bake for 20 minutes. Then remove cover, and bake 10 minutes longer until the sauce is bubbly and crisp.

Yield: 4 servings.

Spinach Chestnut Ring

1¼ lb. spinach
1 cup chopped onion
2 Tbsp. olive oil
2 Tbsp. lemon juice
2 tsp. salt
½ tsp. nutmeg
1½ lb. tofu
2 cups chestnuts, cooked and chopped

Yield: 6 servings.

Preheat oven to 350°.

Chop 4 oz. of spinach, and set aside. Then thoroughly blend or process the remaining spinach and all other ingredients, except the chestnuts, adding the tofu piece by piece to the other ingredients.

Add the chopped chestnuts and chopped spinach. Stir to mix.

Bake in a covered, well-oiled ring mold for 45 minutes.

Unmold ring, and serve with Tofu Lemon Cream (p. 99) or sour cream.

Note: To prepare chestnuts, cover about 35 chestnuts with boiling water, then simmer for 20 to 25 minutes. Drain and cover with warm tap water. With a knife, remove the shells and the inner brown skin, setting aside the nut meats.

Tofu Stuffed Peppers

1 carrot, minced
3 Tbsp. olive oil
1 medium onion, minced
1 to 2 cloves garlic, minced
4 medium green peppers
1 lb. tofu, squeezed then mashed
¼ cup wheat germ
¼ cup whole wheat bread crumbs
1 tsp. basil
1 tsp. oregano
1 tsp. salt
1 16-oz. can tomatoes
1 6-oz. can tomato paste
¼ cup dry red wine
⅛ tsp. pepper, or to taste
1 egg slightly beaten
½ cup Parmesan or Romano cheese

Preheat oven to 325°.

Sauté the carrot for 5 minutes in 2 Tbsp. olive oil, then add the minced onion and garlic, and sauté for 5 minutes more. Set aside.

Cut off the tops of the green peppers, remove the seeds, and wash the peppers. Steam them for 5 minutes.

Return to the sautéed vegetables. Put half of them in a blender, leaving the remaining half in the pan.

To the vegetables in the frying pan, add the remaining 1 Tbsp. of olive oil, the mashed tofu, wheat germ, bread crumbs, ½ tsp. basil, ½ tsp. oregano, and ½ tsp. salt. Cook over medium heat for 10 minutes, stirring constantly to avoid scorching the vegetables. If necessary, add a bit more oil, a tsp. at a time. Set aside to cool slightly.

To prepare the sauce, add the canned tomatoes, tomato paste, and wine to the vegetables in the blender. Blend to a purée, adding the remaining ½ tsp. each of basil, oregano, salt and ⅛ tsp. pepper while the blender is on.

Add 1 cup of the sauce to the tofu mixture in the frying pan. Mix in the beaten egg and ¼ cup of the cheese.

Fill the peppers with the tofu mixture, being careful not to overstuff them, as the filling will expand slightly during cooking. Place the filled peppers in a lightly buttered 2-quart casserole. Pour the remaining sauce over the stuffed peppers.

Bake covered for 40 minutes until the stuffing is heated through and the peppers are soft. During the last 5 minutes, top each pepper with 1 Tbsp. Parmesan or Romano cheese. When the cheese has melted, the peppers are ready to serve.

Yield: 4 servings.

Chinese Rainbow Stew

I often prepare this stew in the fall just because the colors match the season so well, and it just hits the spot on a brisk autumn day. Additional vegetables such as corn, peas and broccoli may also be added if available. Thanks to the Regular Restaurant in Rochester for this recipe.

1½ lb. tofu
⅓ cup safflower oil
3 cloves fresh garlic, grated
1 Tbsp. grated fresh ginger root
2½ cups carrots, thinly sliced
1 large onion, chopped
2 sweet red peppers, sliced
2½ cups fresh mushrooms, halved
1⅓ cups water or vegetable stock
⅓ cup mugi (barley) or brown rice miso
2½ Tbsp. natural soy sauce or tamari
2½ Tbsp. honey
2½ Tbsp. cashew, almond, or peanut butter
1½ tsp. wine vinegar
1 Tbsp. arrowroot, dissolved in ½ cup water

Yield: 6 servings.

Press tofu (p. 22).

Heat safflower oil in a large iron skillet or wok and sauté the garlic and ginger lightly. Add the remaining vegetables to the skillet in the following order, sautéing until they are cooked but still slightly crunchy: carrots, onion, red peppers, mushrooms. Set aside and make sauce.

Combine 1⅓ cups water or stock, the miso, soy sauce, honey, nut butter and wine vinegar in a blender and blend until smooth. Add to sautéed vegetables.

Cut pressed tofu into ½-inch cubes and add to vegetables and sauce. Heat, stirring gently so as to not tear the tofu. When entire mixture is hot, add dissolved arrowroot and continue to stir until sauce has thickened. Take care not to boil mixture in order to enjoy the full flavor and nutritional value of the miso.

Serve as is, with rice, or your favorite noodles.

Twice Baked Potatoes

The basic recipe is suitable for people who do not or cannot eat dairy products. There are variations below, some of which call for the use of dairy products, which you may also like to try.

6 baking potatoes
5 to 6 cups sliced mushrooms
3 Tbsp. butter or oil
2 cups mashed tofu
$\frac{1}{2}$ to $\frac{3}{4}$ cups soymilk
1 tsp. salt
$\frac{1}{2}$ tsp. onion powder
$\frac{1}{2}$ tsp. garlic powder
chopped parsley as garnish

Bake the potatoes in a 400° oven until a fork inserted comes out easily (about 40 to 60 minutes).

Sauté the sliced mushrooms in butter or oil until just tender.

In a large mixing bowl, combine the mushrooms, tofu, soymilk, salt, onion powder, and garlic powder. (Depending on the size of the potatoes you use, you may wish to use more or less soymilk.)

When the potatoes are done, slit them in half lengthwise. Remove the pulp without breaking the skin. Mix the pulp with the tofu-mushroom mixture. Then heap into the potato shells.

Put the filled potato shells into a pan or onto a baking sheet. Return to the oven, and bake for 30 to 45 minutes, or until the tops are brown.

Top with chopped parsley, and serve hot.

Variations:
1. Cut down the tofu called for to 1 or 1½ cups and add ½ to 1 cup grated sharp Cheddar cheese.

2. Choose your own combinations of these additional seasonings:

⅛ to ¼ tsp. pepper
½ tsp. dill
1 Tbsp. chives
pinch of curry powder

3. Substitute 3 to 4 Tbsp. of sour cream for ¼ cup soymilk.

4. Top filling with a slice of bacon. Bake and serve garnished with fresh parsley.

5. Before baking, brush tops with olive oil, melted soy margarine or butter.

Yield: 6 servings.

Tofu Latkes

This recipe makes many potato pancakes, but you will find that they disappear quickly. They are good heated up the next day, too, and can be eaten at any time with a variety of companion dishes, from apple sauce or sour cream to a tossed vegetable salad.

2½ lb. potatoes, coarsely grated
1 lb. tofu
7 eggs, beaten
¼ cup and 2 Tbsp. flour
1 Tbsp. and 1 tsp. salt
¾ cup grated onion (1 medium onion)
1 tsp. garlic powder
oil for frying (approx. ⅓ cup)

Remove excess moisture from the grated potatoes by blotting them dry with a towel, by wrapping them in a towel and squeezing them, or by picking up a handful at a time and squeezing out the liquid. Break up the tofu with a pastry blender for a finely crumbled texture. Setting the oil aside for frying, mix all other ingredients together thoroughly.

Pour the oil into a skillet. There should be ¼ inch of oil in the skillet, and it should be hot before you begin to fry the latkes. Taking care not to burn yourself with the oil, place heaping spoonfuls of the mixture into the skillet. The patties should be about ¼ inch thick and 4 to 6 inches across.

Brown one side, then turn, and brown the other side until crisp. To keep them warm until all the batter is cooked, place them in a 200° oven on a rack above a large baking dish or a cookie sheet.

Serve hot with Tofu Lemon Cream (p. 99), sour cream or apple sauce.

Yield: 6 to 8 servings.

Mushroom Tofu Pie

This pie is ideally suited to a light summer meal in the middle of tomato season. The pie's lightness is due to its having no binder ingredients like cream, cheese or eggs, and it is a treat for people who cannot eat those foods, and for tarragon-lovers, too.

CRUST: (Makes 2 8-inch crusts. To make one, divide this recipe in half.)

1½ cups flour

½ tsp. salt

½ cup soy margarine or butter

⅓ cup ice water

FILLING: (for 1 pie)

2 small onions, sliced in rings

¾ tsp. salt

4 Tbsp. olive oil

3½ cups sliced mushrooms

2 Tbsp. parsley, chopped

¼ tsp. pepper

1 tsp. tarragon

8 oz. tofu, finely chopped

2 medium tomatoes, sliced

salt to sprinkle on tomatoes

Yield: 1 8-inch pie.

To make the crust, sift together the flour and salt. Cut in the soy margarine or butter using two knives, a pastry blender or food processor. When the mixture has the consistency of cornmeal, sprinkle in the ice water, and blend it lightly. Form the dough into a ball, and chill for one hour.

Preheat the oven to 350°.

Roll out the chilled dough, and line an 8-inch pie pan with it. Prick dough with a fork. Pre-bake the pie shell for 20 minutes.

In making the filling, first sauté the onions with ¼ tsp. salt in 2 Tbsp. of olive oil until they are transparent. Arrange the sautéed onion rings on the bottom of the pie shell.

Sauté the mushrooms in the remaining 2 Tbsp. of olive oil. Add the parsley, the remaining ½ tsp. salt, pepper, tarragon, and tofu and mix well. Pile this mixture on top of the onions.

Sprinkle the sliced tomatoes with salt, and layer them on top of the tofu mix.

Bake for 15 minutes, or until the tomatoes are just soft. (Take care not to bake the pie so long that the tomatoes lose their color.)

Spanakopita

This is a lighter version of the original Greek recipe. For people who enjoy the Feta cheese taste, see the variation below.

1 cup chopped onion
6 Tbsp. olive oil
2 lb. fresh spinach, chopped
2 cups mashed tofu
1 Tbsp. salt
¾ tsp. pepper
2 Tbsp. oregano
1 lb. filo dough
olive oil to brush the dough

Using a large pan, sauté the chopped onion in 6 Tbsp. of olive oil for 5 minutes. Add the chopped spinach, and sauté until limp. Then add the mashed tofu, salt, pepper, and oregano. Set aside.

Preheat the oven to 350°.

To prepare the crust, oil a 9 × 13-inch baking dish, or large oblong casserole, with olive oil. Lay into it one sheet of filo dough. Fit the dough to the sides of the dish and allow the edges to hang over the sides. Brush this sheet with olive oil. Fit another sheet of filo into the pan at a slight angle to the first one, and brush this sheet with oil. Continue in this manner, oiling and setting each sheet at an angle to the previous one, so that the sheets of dough overlap each other fan style. Do this until you use up ½ of the filo.

Add the filling. Fold the overlapping edges of the filo over the filling.

Add the remaining filo in the same pattern as before, oiling between each sheet. Tuck in the overhang.

Slash the top on the diagonal through to the filling in several places. Oil the top. Bake 50 to 60 minutes until brown and crisp.

Variation:
Instead of 1 lb. mashed tofu, mix 8 oz. mashed tofu and 8 oz. crumbled Feta cheese. Cut the amount of salt from 1 Tbsp. to 1 tsp., or to taste. (Feta cheese is very salty; taste first.)

Yield: 8 servings.

Tofu Loaf with Mushroom Gravy

This loaf is easy to prepare and most suitable for festive occasions. It is another recipe which seems to be a great favorite of people just beginning to eat tofu.

LOAF:

3 cups mashed tofu
3 eggs
¼ cup bread crumbs
¼ cup chopped scallions
2 Tbsp. natural soy sauce or tamari
1 Tbsp. sesame oil
½ tsp. basil
¼ tsp. garlic powder
liquid lecithin to coat baking pan (or coat pan liberally with oil)
parsley as garnish

MUSHROOM GRAVY:

½ cup butter
½ cup whole wheat flour
¼ cup unbleached white flour
4½ cups boiling water or stock
½ cup natural soy sauce or tamari
3½ cups thickly sliced mushrooms
3 Tbsp. butter

Yield: 6 to 8 servings

Preheat oven to 350°.

Mix together all loaf ingredients, except lecithin and parsley, and stir lightly with a fork to blend.

Brush an 8½ × 4½ × 2½-inch glass loaf dish with lecithin. (If the lecithin is slightly heated before brushing into loaf dish, it will flow on more evenly.)

Pat the tofu mixture into the baking dish.

Bake for 1 to 1½ hours.

To serve, turn onto a serving platter so that the bottom side of the loaf is up. Garnish with a ring of parsley and serve with Mushroom Gravy.

To prepare the gravy, melt the ½ cup of butter in a 2-quart saucepan.

Whisk in the whole wheat and white flour, and cook over medium heat, stirring frequently, until the flour is brown and fragrant.

Add 2 cups of boiling stock or water, whisking constantly to avoid lumps. When the texture is smooth, add the remaining 2½ cups of stock/water and the soy sauce, again stirring constantly.

Simmer the gravy for 10 minutes, adjusting soy sauce to taste.

While the gravy is simmering, sauté the mushrooms in 3 Tbsp. of butter until just tender. When the gravy is done, add the mushrooms. Serve immediately with the tofu loaf.

Tamale Pie

FILLING:

1 lb. tofu, crumbled

1 cup coarsely chopped green peppers

1 cup chopped onion

1/4 cup corn oil

1/2 cup tomato paste

1 cup water

1 1/2 cups chopped fresh tomatoes

1/2 cup chopped ripe black olives

3 cloves garlic, pressed

3 Tbsp. natural soy sauce or tamari

2 Tbsp. vinegar

2 tsp. cumin

2 tsp. oregano

2 tsp. chili powder

1/2 tsp. coriander

whole ripe black olives as garnish

CRUST:

1 cup cornmeal

3/4 cup soymilk

3 Tbsp. corn oil

1 tsp. baking powder

1/2 tsp. salt

Yield: 6 servings.

Sauté the tofu, chopped pepper, and onion in corn oil until the onions are soft and translucent.

Combine tomato paste with water; then add it and all other ingredients, except the whole olives, to the tofu-pepper-onion mix. Heat to meld flavors.

Preheat oven to 350°.

Use corn oil to oil a 2-quart casserole. Pour the filling into it.

To prepare the crust, mix all the crust ingredients together in a saucepan, and cook until the cornmeal thickens.

Pour the crust over the filling. Spread evenly. Garnish with black olives around the outside edge of the crust.

Cover and bake for 40 to 45 minutes, until crust is done.

Tofu Pot Pie

Pot pies have always given me a special feeling of home, and this one is no exception. It's a great success at pot luck suppers.

CRUST:

1½ cups flour
½ tsp. salt
½ cup soy margarine or butter
⅓ cup ice water
beaten egg white or melted butter to coat crusts

FILLING:

1 lb. tofu
1½ cups sliced mushrooms
½ cup corn, fresh or frozen
½ cup peas, fresh or frozen

GRAVY:

4 Tbsp. butter
½ cup whole wheat pastry flour
2 cups water
⅓ cup natural soy sauce or tamari

To make the crust, sift together the flour and salt. Cut in the soy margarine or butter using two knives, a pastry blender, or food processor. When the mixture has the consistency of cornmeal, sprinkle in the ice water, and blend lightly. Form the dough into a ball, wrap it in wax paper, and chill for one hour.

While the dough is chilling, press the tofu for at least 20 minutes and prepare the gravy.

Melt the butter in a heavy-bottomed pan. Stir in the flour, taking care to prevent lumps. Cook over medium heat, stirring constantly until the flour is brown and fragrant.

Slowly add the water, stirring constantly. Heat, then simmer for 10 minutes, or until thickened. Stir in the soy sauce or tamari. The gravy should be slightly thicker than normal gravy to compensate for the moisture that will be released by the tofu and vegetables during cooking.

Cut the pressed tofu into ½-inch cubes. Preheat the oven to 450°.

When the dough is ready, divide it into two portions, and roll it out to about ⅛-inch thickness. Line a deep 9-inch pie pan with one portion of crust, making sure there is dough to overlap at the edges. Do not prick the bottom crust; brush it with beaten egg white, melted butter, or sprinkle it with flour to prevent it from becoming soggy during cooking.

Roll out the top crust 1 inch larger than the top of the pie pan. Brush the inside top crust with egg white or melted butter, and prick it or slash it in several places to allow steam to escape while cooking.

Put the tofu, mushrooms, corn and peas into the pie shell. Then add the gravy. Cover with the top crust, and press it down the edges of the pan to secure it.

Bake the pie in the oven at 450° for 10 minutes, then *reduce* the oven heat to 350° and cook for 40 to 50 minutes, until the crust is golden and the filling heated through. (If the edge of the pie appears to be browning too quickly, cover it with pieces of foil, leaving the rest of the top crust uncovered.) If you wish, brush the crust with butter before serving.

Yield: 4 to 6 servings.

Burritos

SAUCE:

2 4-oz. cans chopped green chili peppers

1 Tbsp. vinegar

1 Tbsp. olive oil

½ tsp. salt

½ tsp. coriander

2 cloves crushed garlic

5 to 6 fresh skinned tomatoes (p. 67), or canned tomatoes

FILLING:

1 lb. frozen tofu (p. 19)

1 onion, chopped

2 Tbsp. olive oil

1 16-oz. can refried beans

¾ cup sharp Cheddar cheese

10 large thin flour tortillas

2 cups shredded lettuce

1 cup Tofu Lemon Cream (p. 99), or sour cream

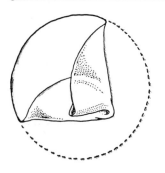

Yield: 10 burritos: 4 to 5 servings.

To make the sauce, put the chili peppers, vinegar, oil and seasonings in the blender and blend until they are mixed thoroughly. Add the tomatoes and blend again until smooth. You should have about 2½ cups of sauce. Pour it into a saucepan, and heat it gently over low heat while you are preparing the filling.

Preheat the oven to 350°.

Now you can begin to prepare the filling. Thaw the frozen tofu, and squeeze out all the liquid. Crumble it until it is about the consistency of chopped beef (you should have 1½ to 2 cups). Add it to 1 cup of the chili sauce, mix together well, and let stand to marinate until sauce is absorbed.

Chop the onion, and sauté it in 2 Tbsp. olive oil until it is translucent. Add the marinated tofu, and continue cooking and stirring over medium heat until the tofu begins to brown. Add the beans and cheese, and mix well. Continue cooking to heat the filling through.

Meanwhile, wrap the stack of tortillas tightly in foil, and heat them for 10 minutes in a 350° oven. When the filling is ready, place about 4 Tbsp. of filling on a warm tortilla just below the centre nearest you. Fold the edge nearest you over the filling then fold the right edge toward the center. The two folds will intersect at a right angle. Now roll up the tortilla. One side will be sealed and the other open.

Serve burritos on a bed of shredded lettuce topped with chili sauce and a dab of Tofu Lemon Cream or sour cream.

Manicotti

One of our favorite recipes. Often people have very specific ideas about Italian tomato sauce. Feel free to add or subtract ingredients. Be sure to cover the manicotti tightly with foil so that no sauce evaporates while it is in the oven.

FILLING:

10 oz. spinach

¼ cup olive oil

2 cups mashed tofu

2 eggs, beaten

1 clove garlic, pressed

1 tsp. salt

¼ tsp. pepper

SAUCE:

2 small onions, chopped

2 cloves garlic, chopped

¼ cup olive oil

2 28-oz. cans tomatoes, drained

½ cup dry red wine

1 Tbsp. basil

1½ tsp. salt

1 tsp. oregano

1 tsp. thyme

16 manicotti shells (approximately)

chopped fresh parsley, as garnish

Yield: 4 to 6 servings.

Preheat oven to 350°.

Sauté the spinach in the olive oil until limp. Chop finely.

Combine the tofu, beaten eggs, garlic, salt and pepper. Add the chopped spinach to this mixture and set aside.

To prepare the sauce, sauté the chopped onions and garlic in the olive oil for 5 minutes. Add the drained tomatoes to the onions, breaking up the tomatoes with a spoon. Simmer uncovered for 30 minutes. Add the wine, basil, salt, oregano and thyme, and simmer for 5 more minutes.

Stuff the manicotti shells with the spinach-tofu mixture.

Pour one cup or so of the sauce into the bottom of a 9 × 13-inch baking pan or dish.

Arrange the stuffed manicotti over the sauce.

Top with the remainder of the sauce, cover with foil, and bake for 35 to 45 minutes.

Remove from the oven, top with chopped parsley, and serve hot.

Calzone

These Italian turnovers are fun to make, a great hit with guests and children and are as tasty the next day as they are on the day they were made. In our house, they are a favorite for picnics. You may wish to make 6 or 8 turnovers, since the 4 here are quite large.

CRUST:

1 Tbsp. or 1 package yeast

1 cup warm water

½ tsp. salt

1 tsp. honey

2 Tbsp. olive oil

2½ to 3 cups flour
(whole wheat, unbleached white, or half and half)

egg white or oil for coating crust (optional)

cornmeal to dust baking pan

FILLING:

2 small onions, chopped

2 large cloves garlic, minced

¼ cup olive oil

1 small carrot, finely chopped

4 small stalks celery, chopped

½ green pepper, diced

1½ cups sliced mushrooms

¾ cup tomato paste

¾ cup water (or ½ cup water, ¼ cup dry red wine)

1 tsp. salt

1 tsp. basil

1 tsp. oregano

8 oz. tofu cut into ½-inch cubes

Begin preparing the crust by dissolving the yeast in warm water. Be sure that the water is not too warm, or you risk killing the yeast.

Pour the yeast mixture into a mixing bowl. Add the salt, honey, and olive oil. Beat in the flour. Use 2½ cups of flour for a light, soft crust, and 3 cups for a heartier crust. We have found that a dough prepared from half whole wheat flour and half unbleached white flour produces a very tasty crust.

Knead the dough until it is smooth and satiny. Then shape it into a ball, oil its surface, and place it in a clean, oiled bowl. Let it rise in a warm place until doubled in bulk. This takes about 45 minutes.

While the dough is rising, begin preparing the filling. Sauté the onion and garlic in olive oil for 5 minutes. Add the carrot, celery, green pepper and mushrooms, and continue cooking until the vegetables are crisp-tender. Add the mushrooms last as they do not take as long to cook as the other vegetables.

Mix together the tomato paste, water (or water and wine), salt, basil and oregano.

When the vegetables are crisp-tender, stir in the tomato mixture. Continue cooking until hot, and then gently stir in the cubes of tofu. Cover and simmer for 5 minutes.

Preheat the oven to 350°.

When the dough has doubled in bulk, punch it down, and knead briefly. Divide the dough into 4 equal parts.

On a lightly floured surface, roll each portion into an 8 or 9-inch circle. To prevent the dough from becoming too wet during cooking, you may wish to coat it with beaten egg white or oil before applying the filling.

Put ¼ of the filling on ½ of each circle. Fold the other half over it, moisten the edges, and seal firmly, fluting the edge if desired.

Dust a baking sheet with cornmeal. Using two spatulas, transfer the calzone turnovers to the baking sheet. Slash the top of each turnover in three places.

Bake 25 to 35 minutes until the top crust is nicely browned.

Yield: 4 servings.   Serve immediately.

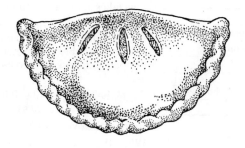

Tofu Olive Pizza

The topping here varies a great deal from the traditional pizza toppings we have grown accustomed to.

CRUST:

1 Tbsp. or 1 package yeast

1 cup warm water

1/2 tsp. salt

1 tsp. honey

2 Tbsp. olive oil

2 1/2 to 3 cups flour (whole wheat, white, or half and half)

cornmeal for dusting baking sheet

TOPPING:

1 1/2 cups mashed tofu

10 Tbsp. olive oil

1/4 tsp. pepper

1/3 tsp. salt

3 cloves garlic, pressed

3 cups sliced onion

1/2 tsp. salt

1 cup dried Greek olives (black variety), pitted and chopped

1 1/2 Tbsp. oregano

Begin preparing the crust by dissolving the yeast in the warm water. Be sure that the water is not too warm, or you risk killing the yeast.

Pour the yeast mixture into a mixing bowl. Add the salt, honey and olive oil. Beat in the flour. Use 2 1/2 cups of flour for a light, soft crust and 3 cups for a heartier crust. Dough prepared from half whole wheat flour and half unbleached white flour produces a very tasty crust.

Knead the dough until smooth and satiny. Oil the outside of the dough, and place it in a clean, oiled bowl. Let it rise in a warm place until doubled in bulk. This takes about 45 minutes.

While the dough is rising, fry the mashed tofu in 3 Tbsp. of olive oil until it is dry, crumbly and brown. Add the pepper, salt, and pressed garlic. Set aside.

Sauté the onions until soft in 4 Tbsp. of olive oil with 1/2 tsp. of salt.

Preheat the oven to 400°.

When the dough has doubled in bulk, punch it down, and knead briefly. Roll it into a 14-inch circle. Sprinkle a baking sheet or pizza pan with cornmeal, and then put down the dough. To prevent the dough from becoming too wet as pizza is cooking, you may wish to coat it with beaten egg white or oil.

Spread on the onions, then the tofu mixture. Top with the olives, then drizzle on 3 Tbsp. of olive oil. Sprinkle the oregano over all.

Bake approximately 25 minutes, or until the crust is done.

Yield: 4 to 6 servings.

Polenta with Sauce

Polenta is a sort of cornmeal pudding which comes originally from northern Italy. It is quite versatile and can be prepared, for example, with cheese cooked in it or sprinkled on it or with meat and tomato sauces. After it has cooled and set, it can be sliced and sautéed or baked, as well. Preparation time is about 2 hours, but you will find its hearty taste worth every minute.

POLENTA:

5 cups soymilk

1 cup cornmeal

2 tsp. salt

1 tsp. sage

FILLING:

3 cups mashed tofu

3 Tbsp. oil

2 tsp. salt

1/4 to 3/8 tsp. pepper

SAUCE:

1 cup chopped onions

2 cloves garlic, chopped

1/4 cup olive oil

1 cup sliced mushrooms (optional)

2 28-oz. cans tomatoes, drained

1/2 cup dry red wine

1 Tbsp. basil

1 1/2 tsp. salt

1 tsp. oregano

1 tsp. thyme

Parmesan cheese

Scald the soymilk. Whisk in the cornmeal, and simmer for 20 minutes, stirring occasionally. Season with the salt and sage.

Divide the polenta evenly into two oiled 9 × 9-inch baking dishes. Smooth the surfaces of the polenta, and put aside.

Fry the mashed tofu in the 3 Tbsp. oil until the water has evaporated and the tofu is dry, crumbly, and beginning to brown. Season with salt and pepper.

Preheat the oven to 350°.

To make the sauce, sauté the chopped onions and garlic in the olive oil for 5 minutes. If using mushrooms, add them during the last 2 minutes.

Add the drained tomatoes to the onions, breaking up the tomatoes with a spoon. Simmer uncovered for 30 minutes.

Add the wine, basil, salt, oregano and thyme, and simmer for 5 minutes.

To assemble the polenta, sprinkle half of the tofu mixture on 1 pan of polenta. Top with half of the tomato sauce.

Unmold the other pan of polenta, and place it on the polenta covered with tofu and tomato sauce. Sprinkle the remaining half of the tofu mixture on top of the polenta, and top with the remaining sauce.

Cover the pan with foil, and bake for about 1 hour.

Serve hot, sprinkled with Parmesan cheese, if desired.

Yield: 6 to 8 servings.

Lasagna

As you can perhaps tell by the number of Italian-influenced foods in this cookbook, tofu is a natural addition to foods of this cuisine. Lasagna is no exception. This one freezes well, too, should there be any leftovers.

2 Tbsp. olive oil

2 medium onions, minced

2 cloves garlic, minced

1 carrot, chopped

1 large stalk celery, finely chopped

1 large green or red sweet pepper, sliced thinly

2 cups chopped or thinly sliced zucchini

¾ cup chopped fresh parsley

1 tsp. basil

1 tsp. oregano

½ tsp. salt

dash black pepper

3 16-oz. cans peeled tomatoes

2 6-oz. cans tomato paste

¼ to ½ cup water or red wine

1 bay leaf

3½ cups sliced mushrooms

1 to 2 Tbsp. oil

2 lb. tofu

6 quarts water

1 to 2 tsp. salt

1 tsp. oil

1 lb. whole wheat or spinach lasagna

1 egg

1¼ cups grated Parmesan cheese

1 tsp. basil

1 tsp. oregano

¼ cup chopped parsley

½ tsp. salt

2½ cups grated low-fat or regular Mozzarella cheese

To prepare the sauce begin by heating the olive oil until fragrant in a heavy 5-quart saucepan. Add minced onion and garlic, turning with a spatula to coat lightly with oil. Allow to cook with the lid on the pan for about 2 minutes. Add chopped carrot and celery, cooking over low heat for 5 minutes. Add green pepper, zucchini, ½ cup parsley, 1 tsp. basil, 1 tsp. oregano, ½ tsp. salt and pepper. Add peeled tomatoes and tomato paste, stirring until sauce is smooth.

If the sauce is very thick, add from ¼ to ½ cup water or red wine, so that it will be able to simmer without scorching. Add the bay leaf and allow the sauce to simmer over a low heat for at least 45 minutes or until all the vegetables are very soft.

Preheat oven to 350°.

While sauce is simmering, sauté the mushrooms in 1 to 2 Tbsp. oil for 5 minutes, then add to the sauce. Drain and press or squeeze the tofu (p. 22).

Bring approximately 6 quarts of water to boil, adding 1 to 2 tsp. salt and 1 tsp. oil. Drop in the lasagna noodles, one by one. After the water returns to a boil, the lasagna will take about 8 minutes to cook.

While the lasagna is cooking, beat the egg and mash the tofu, mixing them with ¾ cup Parmesan cheese, 1 tsp. basil, 1 tsp. oregano, ¼ cup chopped fresh parsley and ½ tsp. salt. Mix well.

Drain the lasagna and rinse under cold water. Spread the noodles with ½ the tofu mixture followed by a layer of Mozzarella on the bottom of a 8 × 14 ×

2½-inch lasagna pan, overlapping the noodles slightly. Spread a layer of sauce over the Mozzarella. Repeat the layering process, finishing with alternating layers of noodles and sauce. Sprinkle top with shredded Mozzarella and ½ cup Parmesan cheese.

Bake at 350° for 1 hour. Let sit for 10 minutes at room temperature after baking to settle. This will make cutting much easier.

Yield: 8 to 10 servings.

Stuffed Eggplant

This is a hearty casserole, but not as heavy as tomato-based eggplant dishes.

1 medium eggplant

FILLING:

4 cups sliced mushrooms

½ cup chopped onion

¼ cup olive oil

1 lb. tofu

⅔ cup finely chopped parsley

½ cup dry red wine

4 tsp. lemon juice

1 tsp. salt

½ tsp. basil

¼ tsp. cumin

¼ tsp. coriander

2 to 3 cloves garlic, pressed

TOPPING:

½ cup grated Parmesan cheese

½ cup bread crumbs

Yield: 4 to 6 servings.

Preheat oven to 350°.

Cut the eggplant in half. Lightly brush the cut sides of the eggplant and a cookie sheet with olive oil. Bake the eggplant, cut sides down, in the preheated oven for 20 minutes, or until the pulp can easily be scooped out.

Meanwhile, sauté the mushrooms and onions in the olive oil until the onions are translucent and very soft.

In a food processor or blender, cream the tofu with the chopped parsley, wine, lemon juice, salt, basil, cumin and coriander.

After the onion-mushroom mixture has cooked sufficiently, add the pressed garlic, and sauté lightly for 2 to 3 minutes. Cool slightly and add to the tofu mixture.

When the eggplant halves have finished baking, scoop out the pulp, leaving a ¼-inch border intact. Mash the pulp, then add it to the creamed tofu mixture, and blend thoroughly. Stuff the eggplant shells with this filling.

Combine the grated Parmesan and bread crumbs. Divide this topping in half, and sprinkle it on top of the two stuffed eggplant halves. Place the eggplants in a lightly oiled casserole dish and cover with foil.

Bake at 350° for 30 minutes, then remove the foil, and bake for 10 minutes more.

Lemon Walnut Loaf with Tomato Sauce

This loaf is delicious straight from the oven, or eaten cold or in a sandwich. If you really enjoy sauces, you may wish to double the sauce recipe here and serve additional sauce on the side. Also, for variety, try serving the loaf with an Italian-like tomato sauce.

LOAF:

1 1/2 cups walnuts

3 cups cooked brown rice

2 cups mashed tofu

1 cup bread crumbs

1/2 tsp. salt

1 1/2 tsp. basil

1 tsp. marjoram

1 tsp. thyme

1 Tbsp. arrowroot, cornstarch or kudzu

juice of 2 lemons

1 Tbsp. barley miso

1/4 cup water, if necessary

TOMATO SAUCE:

3/4 cup honey-sweetened or regular catsup (try Johnson's Table Sauce or Walnut Acres Catsup)

2 Tbsp. water

1 tsp. barley miso

1/8 tsp. nutmeg

1 tsp. dry mustard

pinch of powdered cloves

pinch of powdered ginger

1/3 cup finely diced onion

Yield: 8 to 10 servings.

Preheat oven to 350°.

Toast the walnuts lightly in the preheated oven. Grind them into a fine meal in a blender or food mill.

Mix together the ground walnuts, rice, mashed tofu, bread crumbs, salt, basil, marjoram, and thyme.

In a separate bowl, dissolve the arrowroot in the lemon juice. After the arrowroot has dissolved, stir in the miso.

Combine the lemon juice mixture with the walnut mixture. Use your hands to squeeze the liquid through the dry mixture so that they become thoroughly blended. If the loaf seems too dense at this point, add the extra 1/4 cup of water, a little bit at a time. Squeeze this through the mixture as you add it, taking care that the mixture holds together.

Increase oven temperature to 375°.

Press mixture into an oiled loaf pan.

Combine all tomato sauce ingredients together in a small bowl.

Spread the sauce over the top of the loaf, and put into the oven to bake until the sauce begins to bubble, and the loaf is heated through, about 15 to 25 minutes.

Allow the loaf to sit for 10 minutes after baking; then cut into slices, and serve.

Popovers with Eggplant Filling

Served with a large green salad with a vinaigrette dressing and a light dessert, this dish requires minimum effort, and is suitable for a simple meal or for entertaining.

POPOVERS:

| 1 cup whole wheat flour, or unbleached white flour (or a mixture of both) |
| 1 cup soymilk |
| 3 eggs |
| 1 Tbsp. oil |
| 1 clove garlic, minced |
| ¼ tsp. rosemary |
| ¼ tsp. salt |

FILLING:

| ⅔ cup cubed eggplant |
| 1 onion, finely chopped |
| ¼ cup olive oil |
| 1 lb. tofu, cubed |

SAUCE:

| 1 cup water |
| ¼ cup dry white wine |
| ¼ cup natural soy sauce or tamari |
| ¼ cup minced fresh ginger |
| 1 Tbsp. and 1 tsp. arrowroot (in 1 Tbsp. water) |
| chopped scallions as garnish |

Yield: 12 popovers: 4 to 6 servings.

Preheat oven to 375°.

In a blender, mix thoroughly all popover ingredients for at least 1 minute. Pour into 5 well-buttered custard cups, or into a muffin pan (for approximately 12 small popovers).

Bake for 50 minutes.

While the popovers are baking, prepare the filling. Sauté the eggplant and onions in the olive oil for 20 to 30 minutes until soft. Add the cubed tofu, and continue cooking.

In a separate saucepan, mix the water, wine, soy sauce, and minced ginger. Stir the arrowroot and water so that they are well mixed, then add this mixture to the sauce.

Add the sauce to the eggplant mixture. Simmer for 15 minutes, stirring occasionally to meld flavors.

When the popovers are done, split them in half with a knife and fill immediately.

Serve hot, garnished with chopped scallions.

Sauerkraut Balls in Mustard Sauce

This is a popular dish with people who are just beginning to eat tofu.
Serve with brightly colored vegetables and your favorite dark bread.

SAUERKRAUT BALLS:

1⅓ lb. tofu, pressed and crumbled

1 cup chopped onion

1⅓ cup drained sauerkraut

1 tsp. dried mustard

1 tsp. salt (optional)

2 to 3 Tbsp. sesame oil

¼ cup soymilk

2 tsp. dill weed

¼ cup tomato paste

⅔ cup bread crumbs

1 Tbsp. paprika

SAUCE:

1 tsp. onion powder

½ cup soymilk

2 Tbsp. prepared mustard

1 cup white wine or vermouth

½ tsp. salt

1 Tbsp. and 1 tsp. vinegar

1 lb. tofu

Yield: 20 to 25 balls; 4 to 6 servings.

Preheat oven to 350°.

Sauté the pressed and crumbled tofu, onion, sauerkraut, mustard, and salt in the sesame oil until the onions are soft. (You may wish to leave out the salt called for here, depending on the saltiness of the sauerkraut you are using.) Process or blend 1 cup of the sautéed mixture with the soymilk, dill weed, and tomato paste. Pour this puree into the remaining sautéed mixture, and mix thoroughly. Form into walnut-sized balls. Mix together the bread crumbs and paprika. Roll the balls in this mixture.

Place the balls on an oiled baking sheet, and brush the tops lightly with oil.

Bake for 30 to 40 minutes. Midway through this baking period, turn the balls to brown both sides.

To prepare the mustard sauce, blend all ingredients together thoroughly, adding the tofu gradually to the other ingredients. Pour a layer of sauce on the bottom of a well-oiled 2-quart casserole or a 9 × 13-inch baking dish. Arrange sauerkraut balls in the casserole dish. Cover with the remaining sauce, and bake with the dish covered at 350° for 35 minutes.

Stuffed Cabbage Rolls

2 small onions, chopped

4 Tbsp. oil

8 large green cabbage leaves

1 lb. tofu

1 cup cooked rice

1 egg

2 Tbsp. natural soy sauce or tamari

2 Tbsp. Worcestershire sauce

1/2 tsp. paprika

1/2 tsp. garlic powder

1/4 tsp. pepper

salt to taste

toothpicks to fasten rolls

SAUCE:

1 quart Tomato Sauce (p. 103), or bottled spaghetti sauce

1 1/2 Tbsp. vinegar

1 1/2 Tbsp. molasses

salt to taste

Yield: 8 servings.

Sauté onions in 2 Tbsp. of oil. Set aside.

Carefully remove eight large outer leaves from a head of green cabbage. Splitting the stem end lengthwise helps. Steam the leaves until tender; 3 to 5 minutes should be sufficient. Once steamed, cut out heavy stem section.

Crumble and fry the tofu in the remaining 2 Tbsp. of oil for 20 minutes to expel excess moisture and lightly brown. Add the cooked rice, sautéed onions, egg, and all seasonings to the tofu, and mix.

Preheat the oven to 350°.

Divide the filling among the eight cabbage leaves, and roll up. You may wish to split the cabbage leaves in half to make sixteen smaller rolls. Fasten the rolls with toothpicks; lay in a 9× 13-inch baking dish.

Combine the tomato sauce, vinegar, molasses, and salt to make the sauce. Pour it over the cabbage rolls.

Cover the baking dish with foil, and bake for 1 1/2 hours. Serve hot.

Tofu Ginger Apricot Curry

Many thanks to the Soja Café in Toronto for this delicious and visually appealing entrée. Mango chutney is available in the gourmet sections of most supermarkets, as well as in specialty food stores.

1 lb. tofu
½ cup dried apricots
¼ cup oil
1 cup mango chutney
½ cup cider vinegar
2¾ Tbsp. grated fresh ginger root
1 tsp. dry mustard
¼ tsp. powdered cloves
1 to 2 tsp. salt
¾ cup butter
2 cups julienned carrots (cut into 1-inch slivers)
1½ cups very thinly sliced scallions
1 cup toasted slivered almonds, as garnish
lime wedges to squeeze, as garnish

Yield: 8 substantial servings.

Press the tofu for 30 minutes (p. 22).

Meanwhile, cut up the apricots into ⅛-inch pieces, and cook gently in a small amount of water until soft.

Cut the pressed tofu into 1 × ½-inch pieces. Sauté in oil until lightly browned.

Mix together the mango chutney, vinegar, ginger, mustard, cloves and salt. (Some commercial brands of mango chutney may have to be chopped more finely before being used here.)

Melt the butter, and sauté the carrots. Add the cooked apricots and sautéed tofu. Stir-fry for 3 to 5 minutes. Add the chutney mixture, and stir-fry for 1 minute. (At this point, if you would like a thinner liquid, add a small amount of water.) Just before removing the mixture from the heat, add the sliced scallions and stir in. Remove from heat.

Serve over rice garnished with toasted slivered almonds and lime wedges cut large enough to be squeezed. More scallions may also be added, if desired.

Quiche Tarts

TART SHELLS:

1½ cups flour

½ tsp. salt (optional)

½ cup soy margarine or butter

⅓ cup ice water

FILLING:

¾ cup water

1½ cups mashed tofu

½ to ¾ tsp. salt

¼ tsp. garlic powder

¼ tsp. coriander

⅛ tsp. pepper

scant ⅛ tsp. nutmeg

2 to 3 Tbsp. butter

2 cups finely chopped onion

1½ tsp. flour

3 eggs

¾ cup grated Swiss cheese

To make the dough for the tart shells, sift together the flour and salt. (If you are using soy margarine instead of butter, you may wish to cut down the amount of salt called for, or eliminate it entirely.)

Cut in the margarine or butter, using two knives, a pastry blender or food processor. When the mixture has the consistency of cornmeal, sprinkle in the ice water, and blend it lightly.

Form the dough into a ball, wrap in waxed paper, and chill for 1 hour. Now you can begin to make the filling.

Blend the water and mashed tofu together until smooth. Then add the salt, garlic powder, coriander, pepper and nutmeg. Blend again to incorporate spices. Then set aside.

Melt the butter in a heavy skillet, and sauté the chopped onion on low-to-medium heat until golden, taking care to stir occasionally to prevent burning. This should take from 15 to 20 minutes. Then sprinkle in the flour, mixing well. Cook 2 to 3 more minutes. Set aside to cool.

Preheat oven to 425°.

When the dough is ready, roll it out. Then cut twelve circles 4½ to 5½ inches in diameter. Fit the circles over an inverted muffin tin. (If you are using bite-size muffin or tartlet tins, cut 24 circles from 2¼ to 2¾ inches in diameter and fit them over the inverted tins.) Take care that the bottom edge of the crust is not too thin or you may have trouble removing the shells after they have cooked.

(Another way to prepare the dough is to divide it into 12 or 24 equally sized balls.

Roll out 12 4½ to 5½-inch circles or 24 2¼ to 2¾-inch circles, and fit over the appropriate size muffin tin.)

Prick the shells before baking. Then cook in the oven for 8 to 10 minutes until *lightly* browned. Allow to cool before filling.

Allow oven to cool to 375°.

Return to the filling. Beat the eggs with the tofu mixture in the blender until blended. Gradually mix in the cooled onions and the cheese.

Carefully remove the cooled pastry shells from the muffin tins and place on a cookie sheet. Spoon the filling into the pastry shells, filling them ⅔ to ¾ full.

If you wish to keep the top edges of the crust from browning too much, place the cookie sheet in a larger pan, or cover the edges of the shells with foil.

Bake in the upper ⅓ of a 375° oven for 20 to 25 minutes, or until tarts have puffed and browned.

Yield: 12 tarts or 24 tartlets.

Potato Spinach Roulade

A comment which we have heard in many variations since we began serving this roulade is, "I didn't know you could do things like this with tofu. It's positively elegant!"

Allow yourself plenty of preparation time. Depending on how quickly you cook, it can take between 2½ and 4 hours. Before you begin, be sure that you have a large roasting pan, or a pan of comparable size, in which to cook it, and an ample supply of cheesecloth.

Surrounded by garnishes of fresh parsley with colorful seasonal vegetables or lemon wedges, this roulade is a perfect choice for a fancy dinner party or a holiday meal.

FILLING:

½ cup chopped onion
½ cup olive oil
3½ cups sliced mushrooms
1 lb. spinach, washed and chopped
8 oz. tofu, crumbled
3 cloves garlic, minced
1 tsp. oregano
2 Tbsp. vinegar
2 tsp. salt

DOUGH:

1 lb. potatoes
1 lb. tofu
1 egg
1 Tbsp. natural soy sauce or tamari
1 tsp. salt
½ tsp. garlic powder
½ tsp. nutmeg
⅛ tsp. pepper
½ cup flour, more if needed
flour for rolling out dough

SAUCE:

½ cup butter
¾ cup grated Parmesan cheese

You may wish to begin by steaming the potatoes so that you will not have to wait for them when you are ready to make the dough. While the potatoes are cooking, the vegetables for the filling can be prepared: the spinach washed, patted dry, and chopped; the mushrooms and onion sliced; the garlic minced. When the potatoes are done, set them aside. (Remember to remove the lid from the steaming pot, so that the potatoes do not continue to cook).

When the vegetables are prepared, begin making the filling by sautéeing the onions in the olive oil until they are soft and transparent. Add the sliced mushrooms, and cook until soft. Then add the spinach, the crumbled tofu, garlic, and oregano. Cook until the spinach is wilted, but still a deep rich green. Remove from the heat, and stir in the vinegar and salt. Set aside.

To prepare the dough, blend the steamed potatoes, tofu, egg, seasonings and spices (everything except the flour) in a food processor until smooth and pasty. (Add the ingredients gradually so that they will be well mixed and the processor not overworked.)

Starting with ½ cup of flour, add enough flour to make a smooth dough, stiff enough to hold its shape in a ball.

GARNISHES:

sprigs of parsley

lemon wedges

raw spinach leaves

Depending on the moisture content of some of the ingredients (i.e., the steamed potatoes and tofu), this could be as much as 2 to 3 additional cups of flour. The dough will be smooth, but very sticky at this point.

Put down a sheet, or two, of waxed paper at least 14 inches long. Sprinkle with lots of flour. Roll the dough, sprinkling it with flour on the top, if necessary, into an even rectangle, 11 × 13 inches. Use as much flour as necessary to prevent the dough from sticking. (It may be easier to work the dough into a rectangle by hand, taking care that the dough is an even thickness throughout.)

At this point, begin to boil about 4 to 6 quarts of water. Add salt when it comes to a boil.

Spread the filling over the dough, leaving a 1-inch border at both ends and along one of the 13-inch sides. Leave a 2-inch border on the other 13-inch side.

Starting with the side that has the 2-inch border, roll the dough up over the filling, peeling the waxed paper away from the dough as you roll. This step is a bit easier if you have someone to help you.

After you finish, pinch the seam ends securely together. Now wrap the roulade in cheesecloth, 3 to 4 layers thick and extending at least 2 inches past the end of the roulade on both ends. Tie the cheesecloth at both ends with strings. Then tie another strip of cheesecloth about 3 inches wide around the middle.

Place the roulade in a large, fairly deep pan, or roasting pan, and cover it with the boiling salted water. Simmer for 25 minutes, then turn it over. Simmer for another 25 to 30 minutes. While the roulade is cooking, the garnishes can be prepared: sprigs of parsley, lemon wedges, brightly colored vegetables, raw spinach leaves.

After the second 25 to 30 minutes cooking time is up, gently lift the roulade out of the pan. Let it rest for 5 minutes.

Melt the butter and Parmesan cheese together for the sauce.

After the resting period, carefully remove the cheesecloth and transfer the roulade to a serving platter. Garnish, cut ½-inch-thick slices, and serve immediately with the Parmesan butter sauce.

Yield: 10 to 12 servings.

Tofu Paprika

Be sure that your paprika is full-bodied, since it is important in this recipe. Serve with rice and a green salad with vinaigrette dressing. It's also very good with green beans. Remember that the marinade you have left over will keep.

---

1 lb. tofu

1 cup minced onion

1/4 cup olive oil

2 tsp. paprika

2 tsp. salt

MARINADE:

1 cup lemon juice

1 cup water

1/2 cup olive oil

3 bay leaves

1 tsp. rosemary or thyme

SAUCE:

12 oz. tofu

1 1/2 cups soymilk

1/4 cup oil

3/4 cup marinade (see above)

1/4 tsp. salt

Prepare marinade.

Cut the 1 lb. of tofu into 3/4-inch cubes, and marinate for at least 2 hours.

After the tofu has marinated, prepare the sauce by combining the tofu, soy-milk, oil, marinade, and salt in a food processor or blender, adding the tofu gradually to the other ingredients. Set aside.

Sauté the onions in the olive oil. When the onions are cooked, add the drained marinated tofu to the pan of onions, and sauté lightly. Finally add the paprika, salt and the sauce. Cover pot, and simmer *without boiling* for 20 minutes or until all ingredients are thoroughly heated.

Serve hot with grain or noodles.

Yield: 4 to 6 servings.

Tofu Stroganoff

This recipe is a favorite dish of meat-eaters and vegetarians alike, in all its variations.

1½ lb. tofu

2 to 3 Tbsp. butter or soy margarine

¾ lb. green noodles

1½ cups chopped onions

1½ cups chopped mushrooms

MARINADE:

1 cup dry white wine

½ cup water

2 cloves garlic, pressed

SAUCE:

1 cup soymilk

⅓ cup dry white wine

1 tsp. salt

scant ½ tsp. pepper, or more, to taste

¼ tsp. nutmeg, or to taste

8 oz. tofu

Press the tofu for 20 to 30 minutes (p. 22), then cut it into strips about 4 × ½ × ¼ inches.

Combine the marinade ingredients in a saucepan, and heat. When hot, remove from heat, and add the tofu strips Marinate for one to two hours.

Prepare the sauce by combining all sauce ingredients in a blender or food processor. Add the 8 oz. of tofu gradually to the other ingredients, and blend until smooth. Set aside.

Sauté the onions in 2 Tbsp. of butter until soft and translucent. Add the mushrooms, and cook for another 10 minutes. If necessary, add another Tbsp. of butter.

Drain the tofu strips, and pat them dry, saving the marinade for other dishes. In a separate frying pan or skillet, sauté the tofu strips in 2 to 3 Tbsp. of butter or soy margarine until they are well browned. Then add the onion-mushroom mixture, and cook for 5 minutes. Remove from heat.

Add the tofu wine sauce to the onion-mushroom-tofu, stirring gently a few times. Be careful not to break the tofu. Let the mixture sit for 15 to 20 minutes so that the flavors may blend.

Meanwhile, prepare the noodles. Just before you are ready to serve, return the stroganoff mixture to the heat and cook for 5 minutes, taking great care not to boil it.

Serve very hot on a bed of noodles.

Variations:

1. Marinate the pressed tofu strips in the following mixture. It will give the tofu a slightly more meat-like flavor than the preceding recipe, reminiscent of veal or very tender beef. It is not necessary to heat the marinade.

1/2 cup natural soy sauce or tamari
1/2 cup water
3 Tbsp. olive oil
3 Tbsp. lemon juice
2 cloves garlic, pressed

Combine all ingredients. Marinate the tofu strips for one to two hours. Then proceed as above.

2. Try substituting 1/2 cup sour cream for 1/2 cup of the total soymilk called for above. Add the sour cream in the last 5 minutes of cooking just before serving, otherwise proceed as above.

3. Try substituting 1/2 cup Tofu Lemon Cream (p. 99) for 1/2 cup of the total soymilk called for. As with the sour cream, this should be added during the last 5 minutes of cooking.

Yield: 4 to 6 servings.

Tofu à l'Orange

1 lb. tofu, pressed (p. 22)

orange wedges, as garnish

MARINADE:

1 cup natural soy sauce

¼ cup white wine

3 Tbsp. honey

1 tsp. ground ginger (or 1 Tbsp. grated fresh ginger root)

SAUCE:

⅓ cup marinade

⅔ cup water

¾ cup orange juice

2 Tbsp. grated orange peel

2 Tbsp. vinegar

2 Tbsp. honey

1 Tbsp. lemon juice

1 Tbsp. arrowroot, cornstarch, or kudzu (dissolved in 2 Tbsp. water)

Yield: 4 to 6 servings.

Cut the pressed tofu into strips 4 inches long and ½-inch thick. Combine all marinade ingredients, then marinate the tofu strips for at least 2 hours.

After the strips have marinated, braise them in a large skillet which can be tightly covered. Cook on low to moderate heat with less than ⅛-inch marinade in the pan.

Meanwhile, the sauce can be prepared. In a saucepan, combine ⅓ cup of the marinade with the water, orange juice, grated orange peel, vinegar, honey and lemon juice. Heat to a simmer. Dissolve the arrowroot in 2 Tbsp. water. Add to the sauce, whisking to prevent lumps.

When the sauce has thickened, add to the braised tofu. Stir gently to mix the sauce and tofu completely. Simmer covered for 5 minutes so that flavors can blend.

Serve immediately, garnished with orange wedges.

Couscous Tangier

A variation of a traditional North African dish.

1 bay leaf
1 cinnamon stick (about 1½-inches long)
4 peppercorns
2 small dried hot chili peppers, or ¼ tsp. chili powder
½ tsp. ground turmeric
¼ tsp. whole or ground cardamom
3 cloves garlic, pressed
1 1-inch cube of pared fresh ginger root, finely sliced
1 medium onion, chopped
pinch of saffron (optional)
1 Tbsp. butter
1 medium onion, sliced
½ medium green pepper, chopped
3 medium tomatoes, chopped or 16 oz. canned tomatoes
1¼ cups vegetable or chicken stock
2 medium carrots, cut into 1-inch pieces
1 to 1½ cups deep-fried tofu cubes
½ cup cooked chick peas
3 Tbsp. raisins
fresh parsley as garnish

RAITA:

2 medium cucumbers
salt
1 cup yogurt
2 tsp. lemon juice
1½ tsp. dried dill weed
1½ Tbsp. chopped chives
¼ tsp. garlic powder
Yield: 6 servings.

In a spice grinder or blender, grind to a coarse paste the bay leaf, cinnamon stick, peppercorns, chili peppers, turmeric, cardamom, pressed garlic, sliced ginger root, chopped onion, and saffron.

Melt the butter in a large skillet. Sauté the sliced onion and chopped green pepper until soft. Stir in the ground spice mixture, and cook, stirring, 1 to 2 minutes. Add more butter, if necessary, to prevent the mixture from burning. Add the chopped tomatoes, and cook for 3 minutes.

Pour in the stock, followed by the carrot pieces, tofu cubes, chick peas and raisins. Heat to boiling, then reduce heat and simmer covered for 30 minutes. During simmering, taste, and add salt if needed.

Serve garnished with fresh chopped parsley, accompanied by cooked couscous or rice (see Glossary), pita bread and yogurt or raita and mango chutney.

To make raita, peel and slice the two cucumbers very finely, between ¹⁄₁₆ and ⅛ inch thick. Arrange in a bowl, salt lightly, and allow them to sit at least 15 minutes. Then add the yogurt, lemon juice, dill weed, chives and garlic powder. Mix well.

Chill or serve immediately.

Deep-fried Tofu Cutlets

Deep-fried tofu cutlets can be bought ready-made. They generally come in sizes ranging between 2 × 1 1/2 × 1 1/2 to 4 × 2 3/4 to 1 1/4 inches. In the United States a size commonly sold measures 3 × 2 × 1 inches. Smaller triangles and cubes are also available.

These protein-rich and succulent morsels are delicious eaten by themselves, with your favorite mustard, Worcestershire sauce, natural soy sauce, dipping sauces or chutney, just to mention a few possibilities. Since they absorb sauces very well, especially when lightly scored, they are naturals served whole or cut into cubes or slices with these preparations.

For sandwiches we generally prefer to deep-fry thinner slices between 1/2 and 3/4-inches wide.

It would be good to read through the general information on deep-frying (pp. 23 to 26) before you begin. What follows are some additional points that are important to remember when deep-frying tofu and frozen tofu.

1. *If you are using regular, medium-firm tofu, it should be pressed for 30 to 40 minutes and patted dry before deep-frying. It is not really necessary to press firm tofu. Just let it drain while the oil is heating up, and pat it dry before putting it into the hot oil to avoid spattering. After defrosting frozen tofu, be sure that as much water has been removed from it as possible. Press it firmly between your palms and pat it dry.*
2. *Should you wish to marinate the tofu before you deep-fry it, pat dry the marinated tofu before putting it into the oil, again to prevent spattering. There still may be considerable bubbling to begin with. Since it is highly absorbent, frozen tofu which has been marinated should be pressed to remove some of the marinating liquid before deep-frying. Press it between your palms, and pat dry as above.*
3. *If you are not using batter, slide the tofu down the edge of the deep-frying pan or wok. If you are using batter, place the coated tofu gently into the oil using chopsticks, tongs, or a wire-mesh strainer.*

Remember that deep-fried foods are concentrated, and that portions should be adjusted accordingly. A typical portion of deep-fried tofu weighs 3 1/2 to 5 oz. and contains almost twice the amount of protein by weight as an equal amount of regular tofu.

1 to 1½ lb. tofu

oil for deep-frying

Press whole cakes of tofu for 30 to 40 minutes (p. 22).

Fill a deep-sided pan, wok or deep-fryer with oil to a level between 1½ to 2 inches. Heat the oil to 375°. The temperature of the oil should not exceed 375° or fall below 350°.

When the oil has reached the proper temperature, pat the tofu cakes dry and slide them into the oil. They will sink to the bottom at first, and you should stir them now and then to prevent them from sticking. As they cook they will gradually rise to the surface. When the tofu is floating on the surface of the oil and is golden brown in color, cooking is completed. This should take about 3 to 5 minutes.

Drain the cutlets for 3 to 4 minutes on a wire rack. Pat dry with a paper towel.

Serve immediately with your favorite sauces and garnished with finely sliced scallions, radishes or ginger root, if desired, or use in stews, and with soups or sauces. Some people even eat them with maple syrup or honey.

Variation: *Deep-fried Tofu Pouches*

Proceed as above. Then when the cutlets are done, cut them in half diagonally, and gently cut out the tofu inside, taking care not to break the skin of the cutlet. The tofu can be reserved and used in other recipes, such as the Tofu Cauliflower Salad (p. 93) or in stews, soups, sauces and salads of your own creation. The pouches can now be used to hold a variety of stuffings if regular tofu pouches (see Glossary) are not available commercially. Often tofu pouches are stuffed and then coated with arrowroot and re-deep-fried.

Variation: *Deep-fried Tofu Cubes*

Press the tofu, then cut into cubes. It may be only 1 to 1½ minutes before the cubes are floating golden brown on the oil's surface.

Yield: 3 to 4 servings.

Stew with Dumplings

1 lb. frozen tofu

oil for deep-frying

1 large onion, thickly sliced

4 Tbsp. oil

4 small carrots, cut into chunks

4 small stalks celery,
cut into chunks

2 medium potatoes, cubed

1 large rutabaga, cubed

2 Tbsp. water

1 10-oz. package frozen peas

1 tsp. salt

1 1/3 cups water

2/3 cup natural soy sauce
or tamari

DUMPLINGS:

1 1/2 cups flour (whole wheat,
unbleached white or a mixture)

1 Tbsp. baking powder

3/4 tsp. salt

1 egg

1/2 cup soymilk (approx.)

Thaw the frozen tofu (p. 19), then cut into 3/4 to 1-inch cubes. Prepare as you would deep-fried tofu cubes (p. 166 to 167). Set aside.

Preheat the oven to 350°.

In a large frying pan that can be covered, sauté the onion in 2 Tbsp. of the oil for 5 minutes. Add the carrots, then lower the heat, cover, and cook for 5 to 7 minutes. Add the celery, and continue cooking until the carrots and celery are crisp-tender. Put these vegetables into a 9 × 13-inch baking dish.

Sauté the cubed potatoes and rutabaga in the remaining 2 Tbsp. of oil until they are lightly browned on the edges. Add the 2 Tbsp. water, cover, and steam. When the vegetables are almost tender – about 15 to 20 minutes – turn them into the baking dish with the other vegetables. Add the tofu cubes, peas, and salt, and mix gently.

Combine the 1 1/3 cups water and soy sauce and pour over the vegetables. Cover the pan with foil, and bake for 30 to 40 minutes.

Sift together the flour, baking powder, and salt to make the dumplings.

Beat the egg in a measuring cup, and add enough soymilk to make 3/4 cup of liquid.

With a fork lightly stir the liquid into the flour mixture.

Bring water to boil in a large pan. Drop teaspoonfuls of the dumpling mixture into the water. Cook for 10 minutes, turning the dumplings in the water after 5 minutes.

Yield: 6 to 8 servings.

Drain, and serve on top of the stew.

Deep-fried Breaded Tofu with Coconut Cashew Sauce

A specialty of the Regular Restaurant in Rochester.

2 lb. tofu
½ cup raw cashew pieces
1 cup Lakewood coconut milk*
1 Tbsp. arrowroot
¼ cup water
1 egg, well beaten
1 cup very dry bread crumbs
vegetable oil for deep-frying

Press tofu until firm – 30 minutes to 1 hour.

Roast cashew pieces in a 350° oven for 10 to 15 minutes, watching carefully after 10 minutes to make sure they don't burn. Bring coconut milk to a boil in a saucepan. While stirring, add arrowroot which has been dissolved in the water. When mixture thickens, break roasted cashews into bits and add. Transfer sauce to a double boiler to keep warm.

Cut tofu into triangular pieces ¾-inch thick with sides about 1½-inches long. Bread tofu by dipping first in the beaten egg, then in the bread crumbs. Place on a wire rack.

Pour oil into a wok, deep-sided frying pan or deep-fryer to a depth of 2 inches. Heat to 350°. Fry the breaded tofu until light brown (1½ to 2 minutes), taking care that the oil does not fall below 350° or exceed 375°. Remove tofu from oil, drain, and serve while hot with the coconut-cashew sauce on a steaming-hot bed of rice.

*Lakewood brand coconut milk combines coconut milk and coconut with such fruit juices as white grape, pear and lime. It is available in health and natural food stores, nutrition centers, and those sections in some supermarkets.

Yield: 4 servings.

Vegetable Paella

Paella is a Spanish rice dish which has become an international favorite. The name comes from the two-handled pan in which the dish is cooked and served.

In Spain, paella varies from region to region, depending on the produce and meats available, so if you feel like substituting ingredients do not hesitate to do so. For example, when asparagus is no longer in season, try using pea pods, adding them at the very end without further cooking. Ripe black olives, pine nuts or toasted almonds are also nice additions.

Be sure to use long-grained rice, since the rice grains should be separate and fluffy. Also, the beautiful deep yellow-orange or saffron color comes from the crushed saffron, and is indispensable to the character of the dish.

This meal is rather time-consuming to prepare, but your guests are certain to appreciate it. (It is advisable to cut down the recipe rather than freeze what is left over, since the dish does not freeze well.)

1½ cups deep-fried tofu cutlet cubes

1 green pepper

1 red pepper

2 large ripe tomatoes

1¼ cups minced onions

2 very small zucchini, cut in ½-inch cubes

10 thin asparagus spears

½ lb. broccoli

4 Tbsp. olive oil

2 Tbsp. butter

1 Tbsp. tomato paste

1¼ tsp. salt

½ tsp. freshly ground pepper

½ tsp. crushed saffron

dash red pepper sauce

3 cups vegetable or chicken stock

1½ cups uncooked long-grained rice

¾ cup fresh or frozen peas

lemon wedges, as garnish

As there is quite a bit of paring, peeling, seeding, and cutting to be done, and, once you start cooking, not a great deal of time to do this, you may wish to prepare the vegetables in advance.

Roast the two peppers under the broiler, turning often, for about 5 minutes, or until the skins blister and turn dark brown. Then plunge them into cold water, remove the skins, cut out the seeds and the white ribs inside, and chop.

Peel the tomatoes (p. 67), seed, and chop.

Break off the tips of the asparagus spears, and reserve. Pare the stalks, then cut them into ½-inch pieces.

Break the broccoli flowerets into 2-inch pieces, and reserve. Pare the stalks, and cut them into ½-inch pieces.

Cook the sliced asparagus and broccoli stalks in boiling salted water until crisp-tender, about 4 minutes. Drain, and set aside. Heat 3 Tbsp. of the olive oil over medium heat until hot in a 12-inch paella pan, a heavy oven-proof skillet, or a large lidded casserole (at least 2-quart). Add the cubed zucchini, and sauté until light brown on all sides, about 3 minutes. Remove from pan with a slotted spoon.

Add the remaining Tbsp. of olive oil, plus the butter, to the pan. Sauté the minced onion over high heat until soft and light brown, from 5 to 10 minutes. Then reduce heat to low, and cook the onions with the pan partially covered, stirring frequently until very soft and brown, about 10 minutes.

Preheat the oven to 350°.

Now add the chopped tomatoes, peppers and tomato paste to the onions. Cook, stirring constantly, for 3 minutes. Stir in the salt, freshly ground pepper, the crushed saffron, and red pepper sauce.

Stir in the zucchini, the broccoli and asparagus stalks, half of the reserved broccoli flowerets, and half of the asparagus tips.

Stir in the stock, the rice, and the deep-fried tofu cubes. Heat to boiling, then remove from heat.

Partially cover the mixture (leave the lid ajar, or cover loosely with foil that has small holes pricked in it in a few places), and bake for 15 minutes on a rack in the center of the oven.

Stir in the peas, and bake for 5 to 10 minutes more, until the liquid is absorbed and the rice is tender, but not soft. Remove from the oven.

Let the paella stand for 5 to 10 minutes, then garnish with the remaining asparagus tips and broccoli flowerets and lemon wedges.

Serve directly from the pan with an escarole salad, French or Italian bread, Ginger Vanilla Pudding (p. 188), and wine or sangria.

Yield: 6 to 8 servings.

Tempura

Tempura is a Japanese deep-fried speciality which should be enjoyed immediately while it is still hot and crisp. It is served as it is cooked, a little at a time.

Many other vegetables lend themselves to use in tempura, and substitutions may be made according to season and availability. Other possibilities besides the vegetables used below include thinly sliced carrots, cauliflower flowerets, onion rings, cubed eggplant, asparagus tips, broccoli flowerets, snap beans, and snow peas.

Again, if you wish to refresh your memory concerning deep-frying, please refer to that section (pp. 23 to 26) before you begin.

Tempura Dipping Sauces
(pp. 100 to 101)

8-12 oz. tofu

oil for deep frying

1 green pepper, cut into rings

8 small to medium mushrooms, cleaned

1 small zucchini, cut into 1/4-inch slices

1 sweet potato, pared and cut crosswise into 1/4-inch slices

8 walnut halves, crisped in 300° oven for 10 to 15 minutes

TEMPURA BATTER:

1 1/2 cups all-purpose flour

1/2 tsp. baking powder

1/4 tsp. salt

1/2 cup cornstarch

1 cup water

Prepare the dipping sauces, and set aside. (When you serve tempura to guests you may wish to have small bowls at each place containing the different sauces.)

Press the tofu for at least 30 minutes, then cut into bite-sized pieces.

Pour the oil into a deep-frying pan, wok or fondue pot to a depth of between 1 1/2 and 2 inches. Heat the oil to 375°. If prepared in a fondue pot, guests and the host or hostess may all enjoy the meal together , eating the tempura as it is cooked. If prepared in the kitchen, the cook will not be able to be with the other diners at all times.

Prepare the tempura batter. Sift the dry ingredients into a bowl. Gradually add the water, stirring slowly and gently with a spoon. Do not worry if there are a few lumps. Check the density of the batter by lifting out a spoonful and letting it drop back into the bowl. If it runs slowly and smoothly, it is just right. Add water, a teaspoon at a time, if it is too thick.

Dip the vegetables and tofu pieces into the batter, a few at a time. Pick them out with chopsticks, tongs, or a slotted spoon. Let the excess batter fall off, then place them in the hot oil. To avoid greasy tempura do not cook too many pieces at a time so that the temperature of the oil does not fall below 350°.

Turn the pieces gently in the oil until they are golden brown all over, about 2 to 3 minutes. Remove from oil with a slotted spoon, chopsticks or a wire-mesh strainer. Drain briefly on paper toweling.

Serve hot with oriental noodles or cooked rice. The tempura may be eaten as it is or dipped into sauces.

Yield: 4 servings.

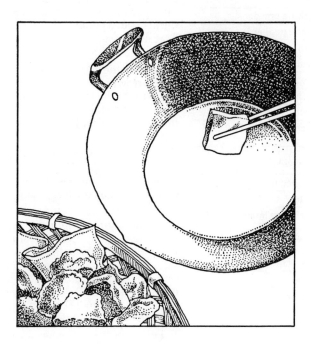

Crispy Beer-Batter Nuggets with Mustard Sauce

These are delightful for an informal meal served with a salad and iced tea.

1 lb. tofu

3 cups strong vegetable or chicken stock

¾ cup unbleached all-purpose flour

¼ cup arrowroot, cornstarch, or kudzu

1 Tbsp. paprika

1 tsp. salt

½ tsp. baking powder

½ tsp. white pepper

½ tsp. garlic powder

¼ tsp. basil

¼ tsp. oregano

1½ Tbsp. oil

½ cup beer

oil for deep frying, at least 1 quart

MUSTARD SAUCE:

½ cup mashed tofu

½ cup water

6 Tbsp. to ½ cup honey, to taste

3 Tbsp. dry mustard

1½ Tbsp. unbleached flour

1 to 1½ tsp. salt

3 egg yolks

¼ cup cider vinegar

Yield: 6 servings.

Press the tofu for 20 to 30 minutes (p. 22), then cut into ½-inch cubes. Marinate the tofu cubes in the stock for 1 hour.

Meanwhile prepare the mustard sauce. Combine all ingredients, except the cider vinegar, in a blender or food processor, and blend until smooth. Stirring constantly, heat the mixture in a small saucepan over low-medium heat until thick, about 3 minutes. Remove from heat; slowly stir in the cider vinegar. Set aside.

To prepare the batter, combine the flour, arrowroot and all other dry ingredients. Add the 1½ Tbsp. of oil, then gradually add the beer, stopping when the batter will flow from a spoon. Stir until smooth.

Slowly heat the oil in a deep-fryer, a deep pot, or wok to 350° to 375°. Be sure to have at least 2 inches of oil in the pan. (For information on deep-frying, see pp. 23 to 26).

Drain the marinated tofu, and pat dry with paper towels. Coat the tofu cubes with batter, and fry until golden on all sides, about 3 minutes. Turn as necessary. The temperature of the oil should not drop below 350°, so deep-fry small batches at one time. Drain on racks covered with paper towels.

To keep deep-fried nuggets warm until all are cooked, place them in a paper-lined pan in a 180° to 200° oven.

Serve hot with mustard sauce.

Baked Goods and Desserts

Fresh tofu's custard-like texture and subtle sweetness have inspired many a tempting dessert. In fact when it comes to instant treats which are also nutritious, tofu puddings are hard to beat. They are fast, and tofu blends easily with your favorite sweeteners, flavorings, fresh fruits and nut butters. You may wish to chill the puddings, for they are generally even more tasty if the flavors are given a chance to blend, but sometimes a person just can't wait.

Just a reminder about blending techniques. If the pudding you are making does not have many liquid ingredients, it will be best for your blender if you add the tofu gradually, piece by piece, after you have put all the liquid ingredients into the blender.

Tofu and soymilk are not only excellent in puddings and pie fillings; they can be added to baked goods as well. They will contribute a rich moistness to breads, biscuits and cakes. Your baked goods will remain fresh longer, too. However, dairy milk can be substituted for soymilk in these recipes.

Do you have a favorite dessert using ricotta cheese? The next time you make it, why not try substituting mashed tofu for all or part of the cheese? With tofu there are so many possibilities.

Apple Coffee Cake

1 cup brown sugar

1 cup whole wheat flour

1 cup unbleached white flour

2 Tbsp. Bambu, Caffix or other grain coffee powder

2 tsp. cinnamon

1/2 tsp nutmeg

1/2 cup soy margarine or butter

4 medium apples, thinly sliced

8 oz. tofu

6 Tbsp. soymilk

1 egg

1 Tbsp. honey

1/4 tsp. lemon juice

3/4 cup chopped walnuts

1 tsp. baking soda

Yield: 8 to 10 servings.

Preheat oven to 350°.

Mix together the brown sugar, both flours, grain coffee powder, cinnamon, and nutmeg. Using two knives, a pastry blender, or a food processor, cut in the margarine until the mixture becomes crumbly.

Press one half of this mixture into a 9 × 13-inch well-oiled baking pan. Layer the apple slices on top.

In a food processor or blender, mix the tofu, soymilk, egg, honey, and lemon juice until very creamy.

Add the walnuts and baking soda to the remaining dry mixture. Stir the tofu mixture into this dry mixture and pour evenly over the apples.

Bake for 20 to 30 minutes until the top is springy.

Boston Brown Bread

¾ cup rye flour

¾ cup cornmeal

¾ cup whole wheat bread flour

2 tsp. baking soda

1 tsp. salt

1½ cups mashed tofu

1 Tbsp. and 1 tsp. water

1 cup soymilk

½ cup molasses

2 Tbsp. lemon juice

Equipment needed: 1 46-oz. juice can for pudding mold

Yield: 1 loaf

Mix together the dry ingredients in a large bowl.

In a blender or food processor, purée the tofu with the water. The puréed mixture should measure 1⅔ cup.

Mix together the tofu purée with the remaining liquid ingredients. Stir the liquid ingredients into the dry ingredients, and mix well.

Oil, or butter, the pudding mold. Fill with batter no more than two-thirds full. Cover the top with foil, taking care that it is tightly sealed.

Place the covered mold on a steamer rack or on canning jar hoops in a pot that measures at least 3 inches taller than the mold.

Pour boiling water into the pot until it reaches a height halfway up the mold.

Cover the pot, and steam for 1 to 1½ hours. Keep the water boiling in the pot, adding more, if necessary, to maintain a constant height of water around the mold.

Preheat the oven to 300°.

Remove the mold from the pot, and take off the foil cover. Set the mold in the oven for 10 minutes to dry out slightly.

Remove from the mold, and serve.

Braided Filled Coffee Cake

This recipe may seem a bit complicated at first, but once you try it, you may find it fun, and once you taste it, you will be glad you took the time and effort.

DOUGH:

1 Tbsp. (or 1 package) yeast	
¼ cup warm water	
½ cup warm soymilk or dairy milk	
¼ cup soft butter or soy margarine	
2 eggs	
2 Tbsp. honey	
1½ tsp. freshly grated lemon peel	
1½ tsp. salt	
½ tsp. ground cardamom (or 1 tsp. ground anise)	
3¼ cups whole wheat or unbleached white flour (or a mixture of both)	

FILLING:

12 oz. tofu	
½ cup chopped walnuts or pecans	
¼ cup honey	
3 Tbsp. melted butter or soy margarine	
1½ Tbsp. lemon juice	
2½ tsp. lemon rind	
egg white for glazing the top	
poppy seeds to sprinkle	

Press the tofu to expel excess moisture (p. 22). By the time you have finished mixing up the dough, the tofu will be pressed sufficiently.

Before you begin to make the dough, let all the ingredients reach room temperature.

Dissolve the yeast in the warm water. Then add the warm soymilk, butter, eggs, honey, lemon peel, salt and cardamom (or anise). Mix until smooth.

Beat in the flour, one cup at a time. Knead the dough for 5 to 8 minutes, using extra flour if necessary. The dough should be quite soft, but smooth and elastic. Form the dough into a ball, and put it into a greased bowl, turning it so that the dough is greased on all sides. Cover with a cloth, and let rise in a warm place, away from drafts, until doubled in bulk, about 45 to 60 minutes.

Mash the tofu in a small mixing bowl, and add to it the walnuts or pecans, honey, melted butter, lemon juice, and lemon rind. Mix well, then set aside.

After the dough has doubled, punch it down, then form it into a ball. On a lightly floured surface, roll it into a rectangle approximately 14 × 10 inches. Cut the dough as shown in the diagram. Brush the center of it with egg white. Save the remaining egg white for glaze.

Pile the filling down the center of the dough, then wrap it by crossing over alternating strips of dough until you have the "mummy" effect as shown.

Carefully transfer the loaf to a greased cookie sheet, and set it aside to rise for another 20 minutes or so while the oven is preheating to 350°.

Bake at 350° for 30 minutes, or until golden brown. If you wish to glaze the cake, it should be done in the last 5 minutes.

To glaze, make a mixture of equal parts water and egg white. Brush this across the top of the braid. Then sprinkle with poppy seeds, and bake for 5 more minutes.

Cool for 10 minutes, then transfer to a rack and finish cooling.

Yield: 1 large loaf.

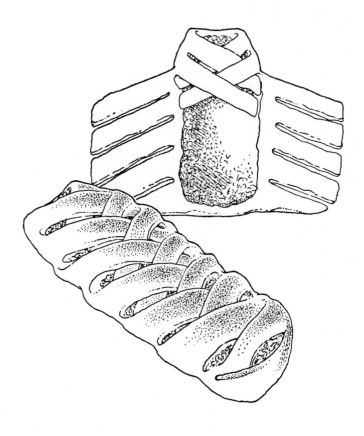

Fluffy Herb Biscuits

HERB-BUTTER TOPPING:

3 Tbsp. butter or soy margarine
1 Tbsp. minced onion
2 tsp. dill seed
1 tsp. poppy seed
1/4 tsp. celery seed
1/4 cup grated Parmesan cheese

BISCUITS:

2 cups whole wheat pastry flour
1 3/4 tsp. baking powder
1/2 tsp. baking soda
1/2 tsp. salt
2 to 4 Tbsp. butter
1 Tbsp. lemon juice
1/2 Tbsp. honey
4 oz. tofu
scant 1/4 cup water

Preheat oven to 425°.

In the oven, melt the butter in a 9-inch round cake pan or pastry dish. Tilt the dish to distribute the melted butter evenly over the entire bottom surface. Then sprinkle the minced onion, dill, poppy and celery seed over the melted butter. Set aside while you prepare the biscuit dough.

Sift the pastry flour; then measure out the amount needed.

Resift the flour with the baking powder, baking soda, and salt.

Using a pastry blender or two knives, cut the butter into the sifted ingredients until the mixture has a consistency of thick cornmeal. Use 2 to 4 Tbsp. of butter, depending on how rich you want your dough.

In a blender, combine the lemon juice, honey, and gradually add tofu. Add a scant 1/4 cup of water to bring the mixture to 3/4 cup of liquid. The liquid should have a full creamy consistency.

Make a well in the dry ingredients, and pour in the tofu mixture. Stir the mixture no more than 30 seconds, just enough time to allow the dough to stick together.

Turn the dough onto a lightly floured surface, and knead for no more than 30 seconds. Fluffy biscuits require a light touch.

Gently roll or pat the dough out until it is a square about 3/4-inch thick. With a floured biscuit cutter, or a sharp knife, cut the dough evenly into squares. Then cut each of these squares into quarters. When cutting the dough, be careful not to twist the dough, or the biscuits won't rise.

If you wish, brush the biscuits with melted butter or soymilk.

Now put the grated Parmesan cheese into a bag; put the biscuit pieces into the bag, and shake them to coat.

Arrange the biscuits in the pan with the melted butter and herbs; pour any left-over Parmesan from the bag onto the biscuits.

Cook for 12 to 15 minutes until golden.

Turn onto a serving dish, and serve. Biscuits will pull apart in small bite-size pieces.

To reheat, cover loosely with foil, and cook at 350° to 375° for about 12 minutes.

Yield: approximately 48 bite-sized biscuits.

Walnut Batter Bread

4 cups unbleached white flour

¼ cup finely chopped walnuts

2 tsp. grated orange rind

1 tsp. salt

1 tsp. cinnamon

¼ tsp. ginger

1 Tbsp. baking yeast

1½ cups soymilk (if substituting dairy milk use 1¼ cups milk and an additional 2 Tbsp. of oil or clarified butter)

2 Tbsp. oil or clarified butter

2 Tbsp. honey or maple syrup

2 eggs

butter or soy margarine

brown sugar (optional)

cinnamon (optional)

Before beginning, let all ingredients warm or cool to room temperature. The flour need not be sifted, but should be lightly spooned into the measuring cup and then leveled off.

In a large mixing bowl, combine 2 cups of flour, walnuts, orange rind, salt, cinnamon, ginger and yeast.

Heat the soymilk, oil and honey in a small saucepan until very warm (about 125°). Do not boil!

Add the warm liquid and the eggs to the dry ingredients. Stir, or mix at low speed until moist; then mix at medium speed for 3 minutes.

Add the remaining 2 cups of flour to the mixture and stir by hand. The batter should be stiff.

Cover loosely with a piece of plastic wrap and then with a cloth or towel. Let the dough rise in a warm place (80 to 85°), away from drafts until doubled in size – 30 to 45 minutes.

While the dough is rising, oil thoroughly a 1½-to 2-quart casserole.

When the dough has doubled in bulk, stir it down, and spoon it into the oiled casserole.

Without covering it, let the dough rise again until light and doubled in size – approximately 30 minutes.

Preheat oven to 350°.

Bake for 30 to 35 minutes, or until the bread sounds hollow when tapped lightly.

Remove immediately from the casserole, brush with melted butter, and, if desired, sprinkle with a mixture of brown sugar and cinnamon.

Yield: 1 loaf.

Hungry Hunza Tofu Pudding

The Hungry Hunza in Portland, Maine, has contributed this recipe, which is a favorite with its customers.

1 lb. tofu	Cut or break the tofu into small pieces.
1 large ripe banana (or 2 small)	In a food processor or blender, combine the bananas, honey and oil.
1/3 cup honey	
2 1/2 Tbsp. oil	Add the tofu, piece by piece, blending in between. If the mixture is too thick, which will depend to some extent on the amount of moisture in your tofu, add water a Tbsp. at a time until the mixture reaches a proper pudding consistency.
water as needed	
2 Tbsp. carob powder	
dash each cinnamon and nutmeg	
1/2 tsp. vanilla	
	Add the carob powder, vanilla, cinnamon and nutmeg, and process or blend until smooth.
Yield: 4 servings.	Serve immediately, or chill.

Carob Almond Pudding

Another customer favorite of the Hungry Hunza in Portland, Maine.

2 cups mashed tofu	In a food processor or blender, combine all ingredients and blend until smooth.
1/4 cup carob powder	
1/4 cup barley malt syrup	Add water or soymilk by the Tbsp. for a pudding consistency to your liking.
2 Tbsp. honey	
2 Tbsp. almond butter	Chill, or serve immediately.
2 Tbsp. oil (safflower)	
water or soymilk	
Yield: 4 to 6 servings.	

Tofudgesicles

Kids love these, and so do adults.

1 cup mashed tofu
1/2 cup soymilk
1/3 cup honey
1/4 cup carob powder
2 tsp. vanilla
1 tsp. coffee substitute
1/4 tsp. cinnamon
pinch of salt
Yield: 1 ice tray of popsicles.

Blend all ingredients together until very smooth.

Pour into popsicle molds, or plastic ice trays, and freeze.

Once the mixture begins to set, put in popsicle sticks.

When completely frozen, unmold and enjoy.

Orangesicles

1 cup soymilk
3/4 cup orange juice concentrate
1/4 cup mashed tofu
1/4 cup honey
1 tsp. vanilla
Yield: 1 ice tray of popsicles.

Blend all ingredients together until very smooth.

Pour into popsicle molds or plastic ice trays and freeze.

Once the mixture begins to set, put in the popsicle sticks.

Unmold when completely frozen.

Pineapple Clafouti

The Clafouti, or Clafoutis, is a kind of thick fruit pancake which was traditionally prepared by peasant families during cherry season in the French province of Limousin. Black cherries and Kirsch or brandy may be substituted for pineapple and rum in this recipe.

CLAFOUTI:

4 eggs

1½ cups soymilk or dairy milk

1 cup flour

½ cup honey

2 Tbsp. melted butter

2 Tbsp. rum

8 oz. canned pineapple chunks

GLAZE:

1 tsp. arrowroot

2 Tbsp. water

6 Tbsp. pineapple juice

1 Tbsp. rum

Yield: 6 to 8 servings.

Preheat the oven to 450°.

In a blender, combine all clafouti ingredients, except the pineapple chunks, and blend at high speed for 1 minute.

Pour a ¼-inch layer of batter into a well-buttered 9 × 13-inch baking dish. Set in the oven for a minute or two until a film of batter has set in the *bottom* of the dish. Remove from the oven.

Cool oven to 350°.

Set the pineapple chunks on top of the batter. Cover them with the rest of the batter, and smooth its surface.

Bake in a 350° oven for about 50 minutes, or until a knife inserted comes out clean.

While the clafouti is baking, prepare the glaze. Dissolve the arrowroot in the water, and set aside. In a small saucepan, heat the pineapple juice and rum to a light simmer.

Re-stir the arrowroot solution, and quickly whisk it into the ingredients in the saucepan. Continue cooking for 2 to 3 minutes, until the mixture thickens slightly.

Serve the clafouti warm, with the glaze drizzled on top.

Maple Walnut Pudding

This pudding is one of our favorite recipes and, depending upon how you choose to serve it, suitable to casual or formal occasions.

½ cup ground or finely chopped walnut pieces

½ cup soymilk

½ cup maple syrup

3 Tbsp. lemon rind

1 tsp. lemon juice

¼ cup clarified butter

1 tsp. vanilla

pinch of salt

1 lb. tofu, pressed or squeezed (p. 22)

Yield: 4 to 6 servings.

Combine all ingredients in a blender or food processor, and blend until smooth. In order not to overwork your blender, break or cut the tofu into smaller pieces, and add it gradually, piece by piece, at the end after you have blended all other ingredients.

Chill for 2 to 4 hours, and serve with fresh or frozen peaches.

This pudding may also be served in parfait glasses with layers of pudding between slices of peaches.

Or try filling pre-cooked tart shells with alternating layers of fresh fruit and pudding. It's also excellent served with fresh fruit that has been soaked in Cointreau or Grand Marnier.

Chocolate Orange Pudding

1 cup soymilk

¼ cup and 2 Tbsp. oil, or clarified butter

⅔ cup cocoa powder

⅔ cup honey

3 Tbsp. orange rind, grated

1 tsp. vanilla

pinch of salt

1 lb. tofu, pressed or squeezed (p. 22)

orange rind, chopped, to decorate top of pudding

Yield: 4 servings.

Combine all ingredients, except the chopped orange rind for decoration, in a food processor or blender. (If you are using a blender, break up the cakes of tofu into smaller pieces, and feed them gradually into the other ingredients already in the blender. The blender should be on while you do this.)

When the ingredients are thoroughly mixed, pour the pudding mixture into four large custard cups or into a 1½-quart serving bowl. Sprinkle the top with a little chopped orange rind.

This pudding can also be put into a pre-baked pie shell, and served with or without whipped cream. In this case, cut the amount of soymilk to ½ cup.

Chill 4 hours before serving.

Peach Almond Pudding

This pudding is best when made with ripe, sweet peaches. It can also be spooned into a pie shell and decorated with fresh fruit.

4 cups fresh or frozen peaches
¼ cup honey
¼ cup clarified butter
¾ tsp. powdered ginger
½ tsp. almond extract
½ tsp. lemon juice
pinch of salt (optional)
1 lb. tofu, squeezed or pressed

Combine 2½ cups peaches with all of the other ingredients in a blender or food processor, and blend until smooth. Especially with this pudding recipe, if you are using a blender, it is advisable to add the tofu, bit by bit, after you have blended together all other ingredients.

When the mixture is smooth, pour it into a bowl and add 1 cup of peaches, stirring gently to mix them in. Transfer to a serving bowl or to individual serving dishes if desired, smooth the top, and decorate it with the remaining ½ cup peaches.

Yield: 6 servings.

Chill for 2 to 4 hours.

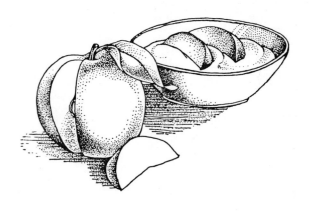

Whipped Ginger Vanilla Pudding

2½ cups apple juice

¼ cup honey

½ tsp. powdered ginger

2 tsp. agar-agar powder (see Glossary)

1 cup mashed tofu

¾ tsp. vanilla

⅛ tsp. salt

1 tsp. freshly grated ginger

1½ tsp. freshly grated lemon rind

⅛ tsp. cinnamon

4 ice cubes

Yield: 4 to 6 servings.

Combine 1 cup apple juice, the honey, ginger, and agar-agar powder in a saucepan. Bring to a boil over medium heat, stirring occasionally to prevent the agar-agar from sticking to the bottom of the pan. When it comes to a boil, reduce heat, and simmer gently for 5 minutes. Remove from heat, and set aside to cool slightly.

Puree the tofu in a blender or food processor with the remaining apple juice, vanilla, and salt until very smooth. With the blender on, *slowly* add the agar-agar mixture, and blend for 1 minute.

When the pudding has begun to set, which it will do after 15 to 20 minutes at room temperature, add the ginger, lemon rind, and cinnamon.

Turn on the blender, and add the ice cubes, one at a time, blending until they have been dissolved. Pour into a serving dish or dishes, and chill. Serve with sliced fruit.

Soja's Whipped Tofu Topping

Pudding lovers will probably want to eat this topping just as it is. At Soja in Toronto it is served with fresh fruit. Try it with gingerbread and spice cake, too.

1 lb. tofu, pressed or squeezed (p. 22)

¼ cup honey

2 Tbsp. coconut cream, or ½ cup homemade coconut cream*

¼ cup lemon juice

2 tsp. vanilla

¼ tsp. coriander

Blend the tofu in a food processor until smooth. Add the honey. Combine the coconut cream and lemon juice. (If you are using the store-bought West Indian or English variety of coconut cream, the process will be one of melting the coconut cream in the lemon juice.)

Add the lemon-coconut cream, the vanilla and coriander to the tofu and honey. Blend thoroughly.

If blending the tofu in a blender, combine the honey with the lemon-coconut cream and then add the tofu, piece by piece. Add the vanilla and coriander and blend in thoroughly.

Chill.

*If you are unable to locate a commercial coconut cream in specialty food stores, Mary Anderson of Soja suggests the following homemade substitute.

Combine ½ cup flaked or grated coconut (or fresh coconut chunks) with ⅓ to ½ cup hot water, hot milk or soymilk, or warmed fresh coconut juice. Blend at high speed in a blender for 2 minutes. Cool slightly and strain through two thicknesses of cheesecloth or a very finely meshed strainer, squeezing the coconut pulp until dry. In the case of soymilk you may have to blend almost ¾ cup of hot soymilk with the coconut to obtain ½ cup of coconut cream.

Yield: approximately 1½ cups.

Orange Peach Mousse

Summer is the perfect time of year for this delightful dessert.

5 cups sliced fresh peaches
1⅓ cups orange juice concentrate
½ cup maple syrup
1 Tbsp. agar-agar powder (see Glossary)
2 cups mashed tofu
¼ tsp. freshly grated nutmeg
¼ tsp. almond extract
fresh peach slices as garnish

Blend the peaches and 1 cup of the orange juice concentrate until smooth. Set aside.

Combine the remaining ⅓ cup orange juice concentrate with the maple syrup in the top of a double boiler, sprinkling in the agar-agar powder while stirring, to avoid lumps. Cook over medium heat until the mixture darkens slightly and begins to thicken, stirring occasionally. Stir in half of the blended fruit mixture, and continue cooking for 10 minutes. Remove from heat, and set aside to cool.

Blend the tofu, adding a bit at a time, with the remainder of the fruit mixture until smooth and creamy.

When the agar-agar mixture has cooled to lukewarm and has begun to set, stir in the tofu-fruit mixture, the nutmeg and the almond extract. Beat briefly with a wire whisk to thoroughly blend and "lighten" the mousse.

Pour into individual serving dishes, and refrigerate for 3 to 4 hours before serving. Garnish with fresh peach slices.

Yield: 6 to 8 servings.

Tofu Cheese Cake

*This is an elegant dessert which requires little preparation time.
We thank our friend Jennifer Taylor for the recipe.*

CRUST:

1 cup graham cracker crumbs

¼ cup melted butter

1 tsp. brown sugar (or ½ tsp.
honey or maple syrup)

FILLING:

3 eggs

8 oz. tofu, squeezed or
pressed (p. 22)

¼ cup maple syrup

2 Tbsp. lemon juice

1 tsp. vanilla extract

4 oz. cream cheese

TOPPING:

2 to 3 cups fresh or frozen
unsweetened strawberries,
peaches, blueberries, or
a combination

1 Tbsp. Triple Sec, Cointreau,
or brandy

1 Tbsp. honey

3 Tbsp. orange juice

2 tsp. arrowroot, cornstarch,
or kudzu

Yield: 6 to 8 servings.

Preheat oven to 325°.

To make the crust, put the graham
cracker crumbs into a blender or food
processor, and blend to a fine powder.
Mix it with the melted butter and sugar,
and press it into an 8-inch spring-form
pan or a 9-inch pie pan.

Rinse out the blender or food processor.
Put in the eggs and whip them. Add the
tofu in small pieces, as well as the maple
syrup, lemon juice and vanilla extract.
Blend until smooth.

Now add the cream cheese, bit by bit,
and again blend until smooth.

Pour the filling into the prepared crust,
and bake at 325° for 40 to 45 minutes, or
until firm.

While the cake is baking, prepare the
topping. In a saucepan heat the fruit,
liqueur or brandy, honey and 1 Tbsp.
orange juice. (If the strawberries or
peach slices are very large, you may
wish to cut them into smaller pieces.)

Dissolve the arrowroot in the remaining
2 Tbsp. orange juice, and stir into the
fruit mixture. Cook until the sauce
thickens and becomes clear. Set aside.

When the cake has finished baking,
allow it to cool for 5 to 10 minutes, then
cover with the topping. Chill for at least
an hour before serving.

Banana Cream Pie

CRUST: (to make one pie shell, divide this recipe in half)

2 cups pastry flour

½ tsp. salt

⅔ cup vegetable shortening

2 Tbsp. cold soy margarine or butter

4 Tbsp. ice water

FILLING:

12 oz. tofu

1¼ lb. firm ripe bananas

3 Tbsp. oil

3 Tbsp. honey

2 Tbsp. soymilk

2 tsp. lemon juice

½ tsp. vanilla

½ tsp. cinnamon

pinch salt

firm ripe bananas, sliced to line bottom of pie shell and for topping

lemon juice

Yield: 1 8-inch pie.

Preheat oven to 425°.

To make the crust, sift together the pastry flour and salt. (Check the salt content of the soy margarine. You may wish to cut back on the amount of salt called for here.)

With two knives, a pastry blender, or food processor, cut in the shortening until the mixture is like coarse sand. Then cut in the cold soy margarine or butter. Using a fork, lightly stir in the ice water, 1 Tbsp. at a time.

If you have made the full pie-crust recipe, divide the dough in half, and roll out one portion between waxed paper. Line an 8-inch pan with it, and flute the rim. (The other portion may be wrapped well and frozen. Take care that you roll it out chilled or the dough will be tough.)

Prick the pie shell with a fork, and bake at 425° for 8 to 10 minutes. Set aside to cool.

To make the filling, blend or process the first nine filling ingredients until smooth. Layer banana slices on the bottom of the pie shell. Then pour in the filling. Sprinkle more banana slices with lemon juice to prevent them from turning brown, then decorate the top of the pie with them.

Chill before serving.

Chocolate Mint Pie

In Rochester, both the Regular Restaurant and The Lotus Café serve versions of this pie. For many, eating it has marked the beginning of their interest and involvement in tofu cuisine.

CRUST:

1⅓ cups graham crackers (or gingersnaps, vanilla or chocolate cookies)

6 Tbsp. melted butter

½ tsp. brown sugar

½ to 1 tsp. cinnamon

FILLING:

½ cup honey

⅓ cup cocoa (or ½ cup carob powder)

4 tsp. vanilla

1 tsp. peppermint extract

½ tsp. cinnamon (optional)

⅛ tsp. salt

1½ lb. tofu, pressed (p. 22)

½ tsp. agar-agar powder

½ cup water

Yield: 1 9-inch pie.

The crust should either be pre-baked or chilled before putting in the filling. If you wish to pre-bake it, then set the oven at 350°.

To make the crust, blend the graham crackers (one package should give you the necessary amount), or cookies of your choice until very fine. (Let your choice of cookies be guided by the flavor of the filling you are using.) Stir in the remaining crust ingredients, and mix well.

Press the mixture into a 9-inch pie pan. Pre-bake for 10 minutes, or chill thoroughly before filling so that the filling does not dissolve the crust. If baking the crust, allow it to cool before filling.

Combine all the filling ingredients, except the agar-agar and water, in a food processor or blender. If using a blender, add the tofu, piece by piece, to the other filling ingredients, and blend until smooth.

Add the agar-agar powder to the water, and bring to a boil, stirring to dissolve. Let it simmer for 4 to 5 minutes, stirring occasionally; then add immediately to the filling mixture, and blend until very smooth.

Pour into the pie shell, and chill for 1 to 2 hours, until firm.

Honey Cream Apple Pie

CRUST:

2 cups pastry flour, whole wheat or unbleached white (or a mixture of both)

½ tsp. salt

⅔ cup vegetable shortening

2 Tbsp. cold soy margarine

4 Tbsp. ice water

egg whites, to brush crusts

FILLING:

¾ cup honey

¼ cup oil

2 Tbsp. soymilk

2 Tbsp. soy margarine or butter

1 Tbsp. lemon juice

½ tsp. salt

8 oz. tofu

5 to 6 cups peeled thinly sliced cooking apples (5 large apples)

1 tsp. cinnamon

½ tsp. nutmeg

1 Tbsp. lemon juice

1 tsp. lemon rind

Preheat oven to 425°.

To make the crust, follow the directions given for the Banana Cream Pie crust (p. 192). Make the full recipe, as you will need both a top and a bottom crust. Once you have made the dough, form it into two balls. Roll out the bottom crust between sheets of waxed paper, and line a 9-inch pie pan with it. Brush with egg white, and set aside. The top crust will be rolled out later. Proceed now to make the filling.

Blend together the tofu, honey, oil, soymilk, soy margarine, lemon juice, and salt. Add the tofu, piece by piece, to the other ingredients in the blender.

Sprinkle the apples with the cinnamon, nutmeg, lemon juice, and lemon rind.

Combine the tofu mixture with the apples, then pour into the pie shell.

Roll out the top crust between sheets of wax paper, making it about 1 inch larger than the top of the pie pan. Brush the inside of the crust with egg white, and put it on the pie. Seal the edges well, and prick (or slash) the top.

Bake for 40 to 50 minutes. Brush the top crust with egg white during the last 5 minutes of baking.

The Lotus Café's Crumb Topping:
⅔ cup whole wheat flour
½ cup rolled oats
½ cup date sugar
(or ¼ cup brown sugar)
½ tsp. salt
½ tsp. baking soda
¼ cup margarine or butter

Combine all ingredients in a bowl. Using a pastry cutter or two knives, cut the ingredients together into a coarse mixture. Sprinkle over the filling, and bake as above.

Yield: 1 9-inch pie.

Almond Apple Tart

CRUST:

⅓ cup finely ground almonds

½ cup unbleached white flour

½ cup whole wheat flour

6 Tbsp. soy margarine

2 Tbsp. honey

1 egg yolk

FILLING:

1 cup grated apple

¾ cup ground almonds

8 oz. tofu

5 Tbsp. honey

¼ tsp. cinnamon

⅛ tsp. ginger

3 cups peeled and thinly sliced apple rings

GLAZE:

1 tsp. arrowroot, cornstarch or kudzu

⅓ cup apple-steaming water

1 Tbsp. lemon juice

1 Tbsp. honey

Yield: 1 8-inch tart.

Preheat the oven to 350°.

Mix the almonds and flour. Using two knives, a pastry blender, or food processor, cut in the margarine until the texture becomes crumbly. Add the honey and egg yolk, then mix well. Press the dough *evenly* into an 8-inch removable-rim tart shell. Bake for 20 minutes until golden brown. Let cool before adding filling.

For the filling, thoroughly blend or process the grated apple, almonds, tofu, honey, cinnamon and ginger until creamy.

Steam the sliced apples very lightly. Reserve ⅓ cup of the steaming water for the glaze.

When the tart crust has cooled, pour in the filling. Top with the steamed apples, arranged in circles.

To prepare the glaze, dissolve the arrowroot in 1 Tbsp. of the apple steaming water. Pour the remaining steaming water into a saucepan, and add the lemon juice, honey and arrowroot solution to it. Heat until the glaze thickens. Use a pastry brush to brush on the glaze.

The tart can be chilled or served immediately.

Prune Tart

CRUST:

See crust for Almond Apple Tart
(p. 195)

FILLING:

¹/₂ cup honey

¹/₂ cup butter

3 eggs

¹/₄ tsp. nutmeg

8 oz. tofu

²/₃ cup soaked, coarsely chopped
prunes

¹/₂ cup ground almonds

¹/₂ tsp. almond extract

Yield: 1 8-inch tart.

Preheat oven to 350°.

Prepare and cook crust. Set aside to cool. Raise oven heat to 375°.

In a blender or food processor, thoroughly blend the honey, butter, eggs and nutmeg until creamy. Add the tofu, piece by piece, and blend. *Stir* in the prunes, almonds, and almond extract.

Pour into the crust. Bake at 375° for 25 to 30 minutes, or until a knife inserted into the middle comes out clean. Cool and serve.

Sweet Ritofa Torte

What is ritofa? It's tofu prepared in a way that resembles ricotta cheese.
(It's a totally made-up name, so don't ask for it in the store.)

CRUST:

2 cups pastry flour
1 tsp. baking powder
¼ tsp. salt
6 Tbsp. soy margarine or butter
3 Tbsp. brandy

FILLING:

2 cups mashed tofu
4 well-beaten eggs
⅔ cup honey
1 tsp. vanilla
½ cup chopped raisins (white, preferably)
⅓ cup chopped almonds
grated rind of 1 large lemon
1 Tbsp. flour
halved almonds as garnish

To make the crust, sift together the pastry flour, baking powder and salt. With two knives, a pastry cutter or food processor, cut in the margarine or butter until the mixture has the texture of cornmeal. Sprinkle with the brandy, and toss with a fork until the dough is moist throughout. (If you are using whole wheat pastry flour, you may need to add more brandy or water. Add it gradually by the teaspoon.) Gather the mixture into a ball, wrap it in waxed paper, and chill for 1 hour.

Prepare the filling just before you roll out the dough, so that the beaten eggs do not have to sit too long before being cooked. Before you begin, preheat the oven to 375°.

Now, to the filling. Combine the mashed tofu, the beaten eggs, honey and vanilla. Heat the honey slightly, if necessary, so that it will mix in.

Toss the raisins, almonds, and grated lemon rind in the flour. Add this to the tofu and egg mixture.

To assemble, roll out ¾ of the chilled pie dough between sheets of wax paper. This dough is difficult to work with, but worth it, so don't be discouraged. Line a 9-inch pie pan with the dough and flute the rim. Brush the crust with melted butter or soy margarine.

Turn the filling into the crust, and smooth the top. Bake for 45 minutes.

Decorate the top with halved almonds and cut-out baked pastry shapes from the leftover dough.

Yield: 1 9-inch pie; 6 to 8 servings. Serve cold.

Steamed Apple Pudding

This is an excellent choice for a holiday dessert. It's lighter than plum pudding, but just as good!

PUDDING:

| 8 oz. tofu, creamed (p. 23) |
| 2 cups shredded apples |
| ²/₃ cup honey |
| 1 cup flour |
| 2 tsp. lemon juice |
| 1 tsp. ginger |
| 1 tsp. cinnamon |
| 1 tsp. baking soda |
| 1 tsp. baking powder |

SAUCE:

| 1 Tbsp. arrowroot, cornstarch or kudzu |
| 2 Tbsp. water |
| 1½ Tbsp. lemon juice |
| ½ tsp. grated lemon rind |
| 3 Tbsp. butter |
| ¼ cup honey |
| 1 cup water |

Yield: 6 to 8 servings.

To make the pudding, combine all the pudding ingredients in a large bowl. Mix well. Then pour into a well-buttered, or well-oiled, 1½-quart casserole dish. Cover tightly with foil. Steam in a large, covered pot for 1 to 1½ hours, or until a knife inserted in the center of the pudding comes out clean. Serve hot with lemon sauce.

When making the sauce, first dissolve the arrowroot in 2 Tbsp. of water. Set aside. Heat all other sauce ingredients to a simmer. Return to arrowroot solution. Stir it well so that the arrowroot remains dissolved in the water. Now whisk the arrowroot solution into the other ingredients. Continue cooking for 2 to 3 minutes, until the mixture thickens.

Substitutions

$\frac{1}{8}$ to $\frac{1}{4}$ cup carob powder + $\frac{7}{8}$ or $\frac{3}{4}$ cup flour = 1 cup flour

$\frac{1}{2}$ cup carob powder = $\frac{1}{3}$ cup cocoa

3 Tbsp. carob powder + 2 Tbsp. liquid = 1 oz. chocolate

1 Tbsp. mirin = $\frac{1}{2}$ tsp. honey + 2 tsp. sake or dry sherry = $1\frac{1}{2}$ tsp. honey + $2\frac{1}{2}$ tsp. water

$\frac{1}{2}$ tsp. salt = 2 tsp. natural soy sauce = 1 Tbsp. rice, barley, brown rice or soybean miso

8 oz. tofu = 1 to $1\frac{1}{4}$ cups mashed tofu

12 oz. firm tofu (Chinese style) = 16 oz. regular, medium-firm (Japanese style) tofu

1 Tbsp. fresh grated or minced ginger root = $\frac{1}{8}$ to $\frac{1}{4}$ tsp. powdered ginger

1 cup dairy milk = 1 cup soymilk

1 cup sugar = $\frac{1}{2}$ cup honey or maple syrup

1 Tbsp. fresh herbs = $\frac{1}{2}$ to 1 tsp. dried herbs

1 clove garlic = $\frac{1}{8}$ to $\frac{1}{4}$ tsp. garlic powder

1 tsp. arrowroot = 1 tsp. cornstarch or kudzu

Helpful Sources

For reasons which I have tried to explain after each entry, the following books have been helpful to me. This list is not meant to serve as a bibliography, but only to acknowledge old friends who may also be helpful to you. I have also included information on one book not yet released because it seems likely to fit this category.

The Book of Miso
William Shurtleff and Akiko Aoyagi
Autumn Press, 1976
Ballantine Books, 1981 (Revised and Condensed)
   As comprehensive and beautiful an introduction to miso as the same authors' *The Book of Tofu* is to tofu. With over 400 recipes. For anyone who thinks of miso only as a seasoning, the nutrition section will be a startling revelation.

The Book of Tofu
Volume I
William Shurtleff and Akiko Aoyagi
Autumn Press, 1975
Ballantine Books, 1979 (Revised and Condensed)
   The book most responsible for introducing tofu to Westerners, and still the most comprehensive source available. Beautifully illustrated and clearly written, it includes recipes (250 in the revised edition and 500 in the original), extensive nutritional information, easy-to-follow instructions for those who want to make tofu and soymilk at home, and much more.

Cooking with Sea Vegetables
Sharon Ann Rhoads with Patria Zunic
Autumn Press, 1978
   This cookbook provides much information about these highly versatile and nutritious foods.

Diet and Nutrition
Rudolph Ballentine, M.D.
The Himalayan International Institute, 1978

An attempt to provide a holistic and comprehensive overview of the field of nutrition. Written for the serious lay or professional student by a medical doctor and psychiatrist who has also studied the ancient Ayur-vedic system and modern homeopathy as well.

The Farm Vegetarian Cookbook
Edited by Louise Hagler
The Book Publishing Company, 1978 (Revised)

The Farm, a spiritual community located in Tennessee, has been in existence for nearly ten years. Soyfoods are the basis of this community's diet. Its members eat no meat or dairy products. The cookbook includes simple instructions for making various soyfoods such as soymilk, tofu, tempeh, and soy yogurt, as well as sections discussing nutrition and the use of soyfoods for infants and children. A helpful book for people with allergies to dairy products.

Food First
Beyond the Myth of Scarcity
Frances Moore Lappé and Joseph Collins
Ballantine Books, 1978 (Revised)

To help us understand what is causing world hunger and what solutions are available to us, here is a well documented, disturbing, and, as Ralph Nader described it, "toughly optimistic" book.

The Joy of Cooking
Irma S. Rombauer and Marion Rombauer Becker
The Bobbs-Merrill Company, Inc., 1975

For anyone who wants a cookbook that provides excellent information concerning ingredients and cooking techniques, well-explained instruc-tions and a myriad of cooking tips, with over 1,000 tested recipes, now including tofu, this cookbook is a time-tested treasure.

Laurel's Kitchen
Laurel Robertson, Carol Flinders and Bronwen Godfrey
Nilgiri Press, 1976
Bantam Books, 1978

For people who find themselves becoming interested in a vegetarian diet, but are unsure of how to proceed to learn about it, this cookbook with its well-documented and very comprehensive section on vegetarian nutrition is an excellent place to start.

Mastering the Art of French Cooking
Julia Child, Louisette Bertholle, Simone Beck
Alfred A. Knopf, 1961

As is the case with any cookbook in which Julia Child has a hand, this one is a sheer joy to read and is loaded with cooking tips. Needless to say the quality of the recipes is outstanding.

Soy Protein and Human Nutrition
Edited by Harold L. Wilcke, Daniel T. Hopkins, Doyle H. Waggle
Academic Press, 1979

The Proceedings of the Keystone Conference on Soy Protein and Human Nutrition held in Keystone, Colorado, May, 1978. During this conference Nevin S. Scrimshaw and Vernon R. Young of the Massachusetts Institute of Technology reported on their research which has found that soy protein used in a well-balanced diet is equivalent to beef in nutritive value.

Soybean Processing Equipment
Jim Hoffman
Rodale Press, Inc.
To be published November, 1981

According to information from the publisher, this book "details how to build a tempeh incubator and two types of soybean presses. The presses not only press tofu, but extract soymilk as well. The simple to build devices enable anyone to begin using soybeans in everyday cooking." Recipes included.

Tofu and Soymilk Production
The Book of Tofu Volume II
William Shurtleff and Akiko Aoyagi
The Soyfoods Center, 1979

This book, based on seven years of research with tofu masters and modern producers of tofu, is an indispensable reference work for people who wish to learn how to start their own tofu shop, plant or factory. It covers all aspects of the business, and provides more valuable information about the different varieties of tofu and its related soyfoods. Recipes are included for popular soyfood products. Available through The Soyfoods Center (p. 15).

The Tofu Cookbook
Cathy Bauer and Juel Andersen
Rodale Press, 1979

The introductory section of this cookbook includes instructions for making tofu in large and small quantities. It includes many recipes for using okara, a nutritious by-product of the tofu-making process.

Glossary

AGAR-AGAR – A sea vegetable used as a substitute for gelatin. Rich in B-vitamins, vitamins A, D and C, calcium, iron and phosphorous, it also aids digestion and has been found to help rid the body of toxic wastes. Agar-agar will set at room temperature in about 30 minutes; chilling will accelerate this process. It will not set in the presence of acetic acid found in distilled or wine vinegars; use lemon juice, apple cider or malt vinegar instead. Large amounts of oxalic acid which can be found in spinach, rhubarb and chocolate can also hinder agar-agar's setting, although cocoa does not have this effect upon it. It comes in powder, flakes, strands and bars. Powder has been used for the recipes here. For 1¾ to 2 cups of liquid use approximately 1 to 1½ tsp. of powder or 1 Tbsp. of light-colored flakes.

Available in its various forms from health and natural food stores, food co-operatives, oriental food stores, natural, gourmet or oriental food sections in supermarkets.

ARROWROOT – A thickening agent that can be used interchangeably with cornstarch or kudzu powder.

BARLEY MALT SYRUP – A natural sweetener prepared from sprouted barley by a fermentation or malting process. Its sugar content is about 65%, maltose being its primary sugar. It is less than half as sweet as white sugar, and the B-vitamins it contains, which increase as a result of the fermentation process, aid in the assimilation of sugar as well. Because it is not as sweet and is more nutritious than other sweeteners, it does not shock our systems as sugar and even honey do. It is an excellent sweetener for tofu puddings and soymilk or tofu beverages adding that characteristic malty taste which many people enjoy. Look for it in health food stores, food co-operatives and the natural foods sections in supermarkets.

BARLEY MISO – See Mugi Miso.

BROWN RICE MISO – Miso made from soybeans and slightly polished brown rice. This milk-chocolate-colored miso adds a delicate, subtly sweet saltiness to foods. Excellent for use during the warmer months of the year when a lighter flavoring for foods is often desired.

CALCIUM SULFATE – Also known as gypsum. The most commonly used coagulant for making tofu today. Regular, medium-firm tofu made with calcium sulfate is generally softer than nigari tofu (p. 209).

CAROB – (or St. John's Bread) A naturally sweet substance usually in powder form resembling cocoa powder. It is often prescribed to people who are allergic to or do not wish to eat chocolate. Unfortunately, in many cases, this comparison has prevented people, especially chocolate lovers, from enjoying carob in its own right. Milder than chocolate with a sweet and slightly malty flavor, carob is high in calcium and phosphorous and low in fat. Chocolate contains nearly thirty times the amount of fat, and both chocolate and cocoa contain the stimulants caffeine and theobromine, neither of which is present in carob. Besides substituting carob for chocolate, it may be substituted for part flour in bread recipes to give breads a richer taste.

Available in bulk in food co-operatives and in packages or cans in health and natural food stores and in natural food sections of supermarkets and grocery stores.

CELLOPHANE NOODLES – Also called saifun, fansee or bean thread noodles. These transparent noodles are made from mung bean flour and must be soaked for about half an hour before being cooked.

Available in oriental food markets or those sections of supermarkets and grocery stores.

CHINESE-STYLE, FIRM TOFU – Sometimes called *toufu*, *dowfu* or *daufu*, Chinese-style tofu has a firmer, chewier texture than Japanese-style regular tofu. Because its water content is lower and it is more compact than regular tofu, Chinese-style tofu has a somewhat higher protein content. Usually coagulated with calcium sulfate, or a mixture of calcium sulfate and nigari. Can be used, without prior pressing, for slicing and cubing, sautéeing, braising, pan-frying, deep frying and skewering. May also be used for thick, creamy dips, puddings, spreads, soups and sauces. If substituting firm tofu for regular tofu, use three quarters the amount, i.e. 12 oz. firm tofu for 16 oz. regular tofu.

CLARIFIED BUTTER – Also known as ghee or butter oil in India and its neighboring countries where it is commonly used in cooking. To make it, melt butter so that the water in it evaporates and the lighter milk solids rise to the top in a foam while the heavier solids sink to the bottom. Remove from the heat and skim off the foam on top. Return to heat until more foam rises, taking care not to burn the milk solids on the bottom of the pan. Then remove from the heat again, and repeat the skimming process. If necessary, repeat the entire procedure again. When no more foam rises, pour the clear yellow liquid into a container, being careful not to pour off any of the solids in the bottom of the pan. One pound of butter will yield approximately one cup of clarified butter. Also known as drawn butter.

COUSCOUS – Fine-grained semolina, the one constant ingredient in the classic North African main course. Cooked until light and fluffy and served with gravies, sauces and stews.

Available in health and natural food stores, some food co-operatives, specialty and gourmet food stores and those sections in supermarkets.

DAIKON – A long white radish, sometimes as long as three feet, native to Japan, but also available here. It is often served grated with deep-fried or oily foods, because it is considered to be an aid to digestion. It also possesses a flavor which highly complements these foods.

Available in oriental groceries or food stores, in some supermarkets, food co-operatives and health food stores.

DARK SESAME OIL – A fragrant oil made from roasted sesame seeds used in East Asia as a flavoring for prepared food. Its counterpart, light sesame oil, prepared from raw sesame seeds, is still more commonly available in the West. Dark sesame oil can be purchased in oriental food markets, specialty food stores, in some health food stores and the oriental and gourmet sections of supermarkets. A little of this oil goes a long way to add a distinctive and deliciously rich flavor to prepared dishes.

DATE SUGAR – A sweetener made from dried ground dates, less than half as sweet as sugar, but able to add a mellow sweetness to dishes. Because of its coarseness, it should be fully dissolved.

Available in food co-operatives and health and natural food stores.

DEEP-FRIED TOFU CUTLETS – Also called thick *age, atsu-age* or *nama-age.* They have a chewy texture much like that of tender meat. Deep-fried tofu cutlets absorb sauces, marinades and broths well, and because they do not fall apart easily, they are excellent as appetizers, in casseroles, soups, salads and stews, as well as for broiling and barbecuing.

DEEP-FRIED TOFU POUCHES OR PUFFS – Also known as age or aburage, age puffs, raw-fried bean curd, fried soybean cakes, tofu pouches or fried tofu. These deep-fried pouches can be split open and stuffed with leftovers, or cut into thin strips and used in salads, soups, stews and casseroles. They are lighter than tofu cutlets, but also have a chewy, meat-like texture. Their protein content is as high as 18% by weight, higher than eggs, hamburgers and milk.

DRIED-FROZEN TOFU – Generally available in Japanese food markets. Can be substituted in recipes calling for frozen tofu. Light in weight with 53% protein content.

FILO DOUGH or FILO LEAVES (also spelled Phyllo) – Paper-thin pastry of Near-Eastern origin. Besides its Greek name above, it may also be called brik, yukka, or malsouka. Because it takes great skill and patience to make filo, many people prefer to buy it frozen. Generally sheets or leaves of filo can be purchased in ½-lb. and 1-lb. packages in gourmet or specialty frozen food sections of supermarkets or in Near-Eastern food markets or grocery stores.

FROZEN TOFU – See page 19.

GINGER ROOT – A smooth-skinned, buff-colored root from the plant, *Zingiber officinale,* used for seasoning dishes and as a condiment. Ginger root should be kept dry, stored in a plastic bag and refrigerated. It may be peeled, thinly sliced, minced or grated. It is often sautéed and added to dishes or used freshly grated in dipping sauces, beverages and desserts.

Available in supermarkets, health and natural food stores, food co-operatives and oriental food markets.

HATCHO MISO – Miso made entirely from soybeans. Its texture is firmer than other misos and its protein content is the highest of all misos. At the same time it contains less salt than either rice or barley miso. It imparts to food a hearty richness that matches its dark chocolate color. There are other soybean misos, but Hatcho is the most well known of them.

JAPANESE-STYLE REGULAR, MEDIUM-FIRM TOFU – The most common tofu available in North America today. Has a softer texture, lighter consistency and not quite as high a protein content as Chinese-style firm tofu. Generally coagulated with nigari or calcium sulfate, it is highly versatile and nutritious.

KOMBU – A sea vegetable abundant in B-vitamins, rich in calcium and trace minerals and a good source of vitamins A and C. Sold in olive-brown strands which can be broken or cut with scissors and used in making vegetable soup and stew broths. Adding a strip of kombu to legumes will provide seasoning, accelerate cooking, and aid digestion.

Available in health and natural food stores, oriental food markets, food co-operatives, some supermarkets and grocery stores.

KOME MISO – Miso made from soybeans and white rice. One of the most popular misos in Japan and suitable for all types of cooking. Also known as rice miso and red miso.

KUDZU POWDER – A high-quality, imported white cooking starch which can be used interchangeably with arrowroot or cornstarch. It is, however, considerably more expensive than either of those two starches. Kudzu powder is extracted from the root of the wild kudzu vine which grows abundantly as ground cover in the southeastern United States. In East Asia it is used for medicinal purposes as well.

Available primarily in health and natural food stores, in some food co-operatives and the health and natural food sections of some supermarkets. For more information, see *The Book of Kudzu* by William Shurtleff and Akiko Aoyagi.

LECITHIN, LIQUID – Liquid lecithin may be used in baked goods as a moisturizer and preservative, as a replacement for oil in coating baking pans and dishes, and as an emulsifier in beverages, puddings, dips, spreads and dressings. Commercially it is often used as a preservative. Found naturally in soybeans, in certain other beans and peas, and in egg yolk, lecithin is known most widely for its ability to break up fats and aid digestion. In some cases it has been found to lower cholesterol levels in the human body. In addition to its liquid form, lecithin is also sold in granular form and in capsules.

Available in nutrition centers, health and natural food stores and is an increasingly common sight in those sections of supermarkets and grocery stores.

MIRIN – A sweet sake or rice wine used exclusively for cooking in Japan. It can be used as a substitute for traditional sweeteners such as honey, sugar, corn and fruit syrups. Sake or sherry with a small amount of honey may be substituted for it in recipes (p. 199).

Available in oriental food markets, specialty food stores, oriental and gourmet sections of supermarkets and grocery stores.

MISO – A fermented soy product appearing in many varieties which have consistencies similar to smooth or chunky peanut butters. Miso is made by the fermentation of whole or mashed soybeans (or defatted soybean meal) with some of the soybeans or a grain, rice or barley, serving as the growing bed for the spores or fermenting agents. Water and a little salt is added to this and then depending on the varieties, which range from almost intoxicatingly sweet to robust and salty, fermentation will be as short as a few days or as long as three years. The regular misos which are those with longer fermentation times and a variety of hearty, salty flavors are Kome or red (rice), Mugi (barley) and Hatcho (soybean) miso. Brown rice miso is a type becoming increasingly popular in the West. See individual entries for more information.

Miso is very high in protein; it contains natural enzymes, micro-organisms and lactic acid bacteria also found in yogurt, which aid digestion and can help relieve indigestion as well. It is a good source of B-vitamins, especially vitamin B_{12} which is important for people who do not eat meat or dairy products. Research by the Japanese has shown that miso contains a substance called zybecolin which can attract, absorb and help the body discharge radioactive wastes. For people who wish to restrict their intake of salt, miso is excellent. Like salt it brings out the flavor in foods while being on the average only 12% salt (for substitutions see page 199). When you add miso to flavor foods you are adding high-quality protein, too. Try it in soups, sauces, stews, broths; it is often used in dressings, dips, spreads and desserts as well.

Miso should not be boiled, because boiling destroys its healthful micro-organisms and enzymes, thereby decreasing its nutritional value.

The regular misos (rice, barley and soybean) are generally available in bulk from food co-operatives or packaged from health and natural food stores as well as those sections in some supermarkets. At times it is also packaged as soybean paste. The sweet misos are more likely to be found in oriental food markets. For the recipes in this book, Hatcho, brown rice and mugi miso have been used. Miso is also now being made in North America. Do not hesitate to experiment with these as well. For more information and recipes see *The Book of Miso* by William Shurtleff and Akiko Aoyagi.

MUGI MISO – Miso made from soybeans and barley, ranging in texture from chunky to smooth with longer fermentation and in colour from reddish brown to deep chocolate brown. Ideal for use in soups; its flavor is deep and rich.

NATURAL SOY SAUCE – A fermented seasoning made from equal parts of whole soybeans and roasted cracked wheat, some salt, water and fermenting agents which have been allowed to ferment slowly and naturally. It is pasteurized but contains no additives and preservatives. Regular fermented soy sauce is made from defatted soybean meal rather than whole soybeans under a considerably shorter temperature-controlled fermentation process. It is lower in price, but compares favorably in taste with the more expensive natural soy sauce. Kikkoman makes a fine regular soy sauce.

There is a vast difference between the fermented soy sauces and the *synthetic* versions produced in the United States usually bearing Chinese names. When you are buying soy sauce, be sure to check the label and if such ingredients as hydrolized vegetable protein, corn syrup, or caramel coloring agents appear, do not purchase such brands for seasoning the recipes in this book. We have used natural soy sauce and tamari (See p. 212) in our recipes and the substitution of synthetic soy sauce will make a significant difference in taste and possibly also give the dish a higher salt content. Natural soy sauce is only 18% salt (see page 199 for substitutions).

Natural soy sauce may be found in health and natural food stores, food co-operatives, oriental and natural food sections of large supermarkets and grocery stores. Regular fermented soy sauces can now be found in food stores of almost every description.

NIGARI – Also known as bittern, the by-product of table salt extraction from sea water. Although it is composed mainly of magnesium chloride, it contains other salts and minerals present in sea water. Nigari is a popular coagulant used in making tofu.

NORI – Of all the sea vegetables, one of the richest in protein and as high in vitamin A as carrots; also rich in vitamin C and the B-vitamins as well as calcium, magnesium and phosphorous. It is cholesterol-free and can also help reduce the body's cholesterol levels. Nori is often served with deep-fried foods, because it can aid digestion. It is eaten as is or crisped (p. 50), torn or cut for salads and stir-fry dishes, crumbled and dusted as a seasoning or used as a wrapping for rice, vegetables and tofu. It is delicious crisped and dipped into soy sauce or mustard.

Packaged in green, purplish or olive-brown sheets, it is available in health and natural food stores, oriental food markets, food co-operatives, some supermarkets and grocery stores. Also known as laver.

NUTRITIONAL YEAST – Not to be confused with Brewers' or Torula yeast, this yeast comes as deep yellow flakes or in powder form and can have an almost cheesy flavor when cooked in sauces, gravies or spreads. Fried, it tastes nutty, even "chickeny," and in beverages it closely resembles malt. It is high in protein and carbohydrates, low in fat and easily digestible; however, its most outstanding value lies in the richness of its B-vitamin content. Its deep yellow color, for example, comes from its abundance of riboflavin. The presence and proportion of the specific vitamins will vary according to the food yeast used and the solution in which it is grown, so be sure to check the nutritional breakdown of the yeast you buy.

Available in health and natural food stores, food co-operatives and some supermarkets and grocery stores.

OKARA – The Japanese name for a nutritious by-product of the soymilk- and tofu-making process. It is the soy pulp which remains behind when soymilk is pressed from ground cooked soybean purée. It retains some of the protein content from the original soybean, but it is most prized for the dietary fiber it can contribute to foods. Okara has many uses. It can be sautéed and added to vegetables, scrambled eggs, soups, and stews or roasted and added to granola. It may be substituted for some of the flour for lighter, moister baked goods with higher nutritional value. Okara is very perishable and will keep only about a week in the refrigerator. Generally it can only be purchased from tofu shops or soy dairies where it is quite inexpensive. If you make tofu or soymilk at home you will also have a supply of okara. For recipes and more information see *The Tofu Cookbook* by Cathy Bauer and Juel Andersen, *The Book of Tofu* by William Shurtleff and Akiko Aoyagi, and *The Farm Vegetarian Cookbook* edited by Louise Hagler.

PROTEIN COMPLEMENTARITY – In all protein sources the protein molecules are made up of amino acids. There are eight essential amino acids which must be taken into the body already formed, at the same time and in a specific proportion for optimal utilization. If a food source is deficient in one of these amino acids, this deficiency will cause the utilization of the other essential amino acids to be limited. Generally grains such as rice, wheat, and corn are low in lysine and isoleucine, two amino acids which are plentiful in soyfoods. On the other hand, soyfoods' lower methionine content is "complemented" by the higher level of methionine in grains. Eaten together in the proper proportions their combined Net Protein Utilization is higher than either of their NPU's if eaten alone. For example, 8 oz. of tofu combined with one cup uncooked brown rice has a 32% higher NPU (Net Protein Utilization) than either tofu or brown rice alone.

RICE MISO – See Kome Miso.

SAKE – Japanese rice wine used often in cooking. May be purchased from liquor stores. Sherry can be substituted for sake.

SALTED BLACK BEANS – A highly flavorful ingredient made from black soybeans which have been fermented in water and salt with ginger, orange peel and assorted spices. Generally available in oriental or Chinese food markets. Also known as fermented black beans.

SAVORY-BAKED OR SAVORY-PRESSED TOFU – Tofu that has been pressed and marinated in soy sauce and seasonings and then baked. Can be added to soups, salads or main dishes that call for a pressed and marinated tofu. Contains 20 to 23% protein.

SESAME BUTTER – A darker, thicker product than tahini made from roasted whole dark sesame seeds. Because the calcium-rich hulls have not been removed, sesame butter is even more nutritious than tahini. (Since whole sesame seeds are difficult to digest, both tahini and sesame butter are excellent ways to consume these protein- and calcium-rich seeds.)

Available in health and natural food stores, food co-operatives and some supermarkets and grocery stores.

SESAME OIL – See Dark Sesame Oil.

SHOYU – The Japanese word for soy sauce which is being used in the West as well. See natural soy sauce.

SOYBEAN MISO – See Hatcho Miso.

SOYMILK – Besides being the milk which is coagulated to make tofu, this liquid, pressed from ground, cooked soybeans, has outstanding qualities of its own. Its protein content is higher than dairy milk's, and although its calcium is lower, this may be counterbalanced by several things: its iron content is considerably higher, it contains no cholesterol, next to no sodium, and is low in fat. It also contains the water-soluble B-vitamins which, in the tofu-making process, go off in the whey. Soymilk is lower on the food chain than dairy milk, which means that it is much freer of pesticides, herbicides and radioactive substances. It offers an alternative to dairy milk for the growing number of people who are lactose intolerant or have other allergic reactions to dairy milk.

Soymilk more closely resembles mother's milk than dairy milk does except that its protein content is significantly higher, and because of this, parents are advised not to feed soymilk to babies until they are seven to eight months old, and then plenty of water should be given with it to dilute it (see *The Farm Vegetarian Cookbook* edited by Louise Hagler or *Vegetarian Baby* by Sharon Yntema.)

In cooking, soymilk can be substituted for dairy milk. When used in baked goods, it has a moistening effect and also acts as a preservative. Soymilk will curdle if boiled, especially in the presence of wine, soy sauce, Worcestershire sauce, salt, or lemon juice. Soymilk will keep from five to seven days in the refrigerator. It can also be frozen.

Available in health and natural food stores, in oriental food markets, food co-operatives, tofu shops, soy dairies and in the natural food sections of some supermarkets. There are also soymilk powders available at health and natural food stores and in some supermarkets.

For more information on making soymilk see *The Book of Tofu* by Shurtleff and Aoyagi; for information on fortifying soymilk see *Laurel's Kitchen* by Robertson, Flinders and Godfrey and *The Tofu Cookbook* by Bauer and Andersen.

SOY POWDER – Also called soya powder. A powder of finely ground soybeans which has been heat treated to de-activate an enzyme in raw soybeans which inhibits protein digestion. It can be used to make soymilk; it is often added to foods to increase the protein content. Be sure to check the instructions on the package.

Available in health and natural food stores, some food co-operatives, supermarkets and grocery stores.

TAHINI – A thick, creamy paste made from ground, de-hulled, roasted or unroasted white sesame seeds. It is a staple protein and rich source of calcium for peoples in the Middle East and Northern Africa. Tahini can be used in a variety of dishes from spreads and dressings to main dishes, desserts and beverages. Commonly available in health and natural food stores, food co-operatives, some supermarkets and food markets specializing in Middle Eastern or North African foods.

TAMARI – A fermented seasoning which for a long time in the West was held to be the same as natural soy sauce, but which is actually a slightly different product. Natural soy sauce is made from equal parts of cracked wheat and soybeans. Its flavor and aroma are more subtle and volatile than tamari's due to the alcohol which is a by-product of the fermentation of the wheat and which burns off during cooking. Tamari's deeper and more robust flavor comes from the soybeans' amino acids which are released during fermentation, but which are not volatile. Tamari will remain to season during long periods of cooking and has an even greater tenderizing effect on food than soy sauce. It is, however, more expensive and primarily available in health and natural food stores and some food co-operatives. The recipes here have been prepared using both natural soy sauce and tamari. You may find that you prefer one or the other depending upon the recipe.

WHEY – The clear yellow liquid by-product, along with okara, of the soymilk- and tofu-making process. It can be used as a plant food, compost material or as a mild soap. When used for washing, the lecithin in it will cut through oil left on utensils. It can also be used for bathing. Whey contains many of the water-soluble B-vitamins, some protein and natural sugars. Some people use whey to replace water or milk in baked goods or for soup stocks and broths. It is not generally sold, but can be collected when making tofu at home.

WORCESTERSHIRE SAUCE – The recipes in this cookbook calling for this common sauce were created with commercially prepared Worcestershire sauces containing no anchovies or essence of anchovy. Brands of anchovy-less Worcestershire sauce are generally found in the oriental and gourmet sections of supermarkets or in specialty food stores. Check the ingredients listed on the label to be sure, if this is a concern for you. Both Kikkoman and Sharwood's market a variety of Worcestershire sauces without anchovies.

Index

Note: For those of you who must, or wish to, limit your intake of eggs or dairy products, the appetizers, entrées, and baked goods and desserts have been categorized as "eggless," "dairyless," or "eggless and dairyless." For example, after "Entrées, eggless," those recipes will be listed which do not require eggs. Since the dips and spreads, soups, sandwiches, and dressings and sauces are almost without exception both eggless and dairyless, they have not been broken down into these categories.